Kids Crossword Puzzle Book Ages 8-11

90 Crossword Easy Puzzles

This book includes free bonus that are available here:
www.funspace.club
Follow us: facebook.com/funspaceclub

Introduction

This crosswords puzzle book contain English words for kids 8-11 years olds. Crosswords is a very easy and simple game. It's fun & educate kids. You just have to have a good stock of words. Look at empty boxes. By default, the game takes you through the clues in order starting with clue 1. After you fill in a clue you are taken to the next one. You have to fill up those across (horizontal) empty boxes and down (vertical) empty boxes with the right words and phrases by using clue to get idea.

See more great books for kids at

www.funspace.club
Follow us : facebook.com/funspaceclub

Send email to get answer & solution here : funspaceclub18@gmail.com

Season

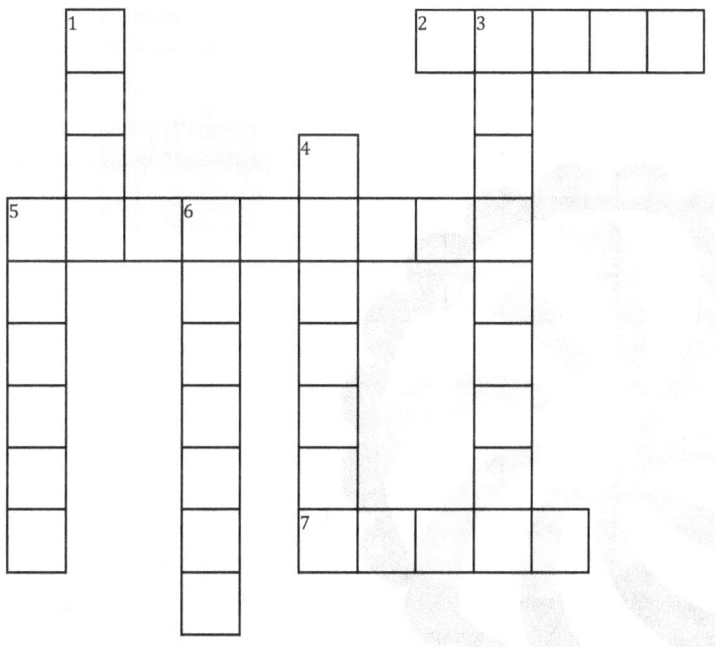

Across

2. I am a baby chicken.

5. _____s are made of snow - they are crystals. No two _____s look alike, but they all have six sides.

7. _____ is freezing rain.

Down

1. Sweaters are made out of _____.

3. Some animals _____ during winter; they go into a very deep sleep-like state during freezing weather. They awaken only when the weather warms.

4. April showers bring may _____

5. _____ is the season after winter and before summer.

6. _____ is the state that the outdoors is in, like how windy it is, how hot or cold it is, or if it is raining or snowing.

Animals

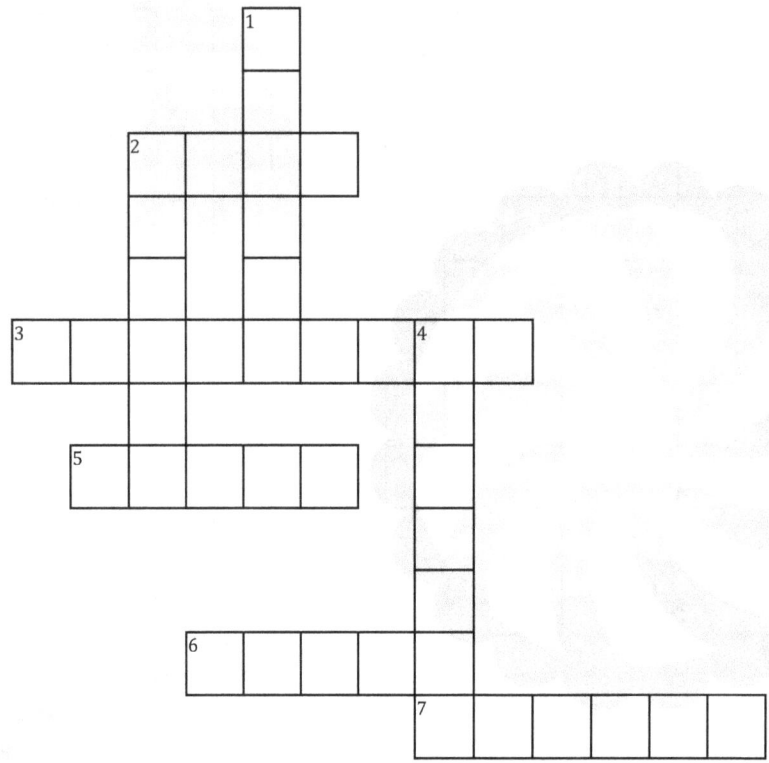

Across

2. A common black bird with a loud call.

3. A flying insect with four large wings that often have bright colors.

5. A large mammal with black and white stripes that looks like a horse. _____s live in Africa.

6. The _____ is the largest of the cats. Like lions, _____s are very strong and fierce hunters.

7. The _____ is a member of the horse family. The words _____ and ass are used to identify the same animal.

Down

1. A plump game bird with dull, spotted feathers. The male does a complicated dance or call for the female.

2. _____ are large, hoofed mammals that people raise for their meat, milk, or hides. In some places _____ also pull carts or farm equipment.

4. A large mammal with short yellow or gray fur and black spots. _____s with very dark fur are called black _____s or panthers. They live in southern Asia and Africa but are threatened or endangered in all their habitats. _____s are carnivores and are closely related to lions, tigers, and other big cats that roar.

School

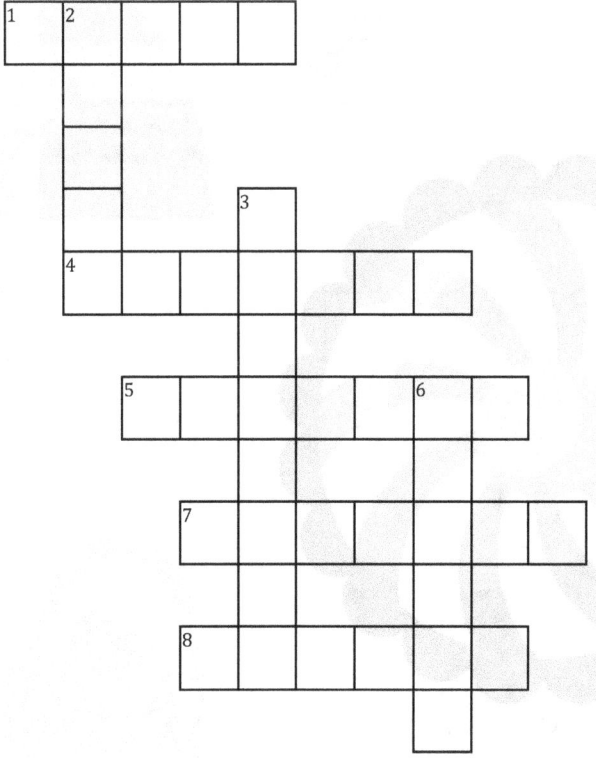

Across

1. A thin material made from wood, rags, or grasses. _____ is used for writing, wrapping, and covering walls.

4. A system of studying, testing, and experimenting on things in nature. _____ is a search for general laws about how the world works.

5. Any activity that takes great effort or planning.

7. A place where books, records, and other materials are kept and from which they may be borrowed.

8. A period of instruction with a teacher, or a specific group of things to be learned or studied together.

Down

2. A book of maps, tables, or charts.

3. To learn completely so as to hold in the memory.

6. A colored stick or pencil made of wax. A _____ is used for drawing and coloring.

Vacation

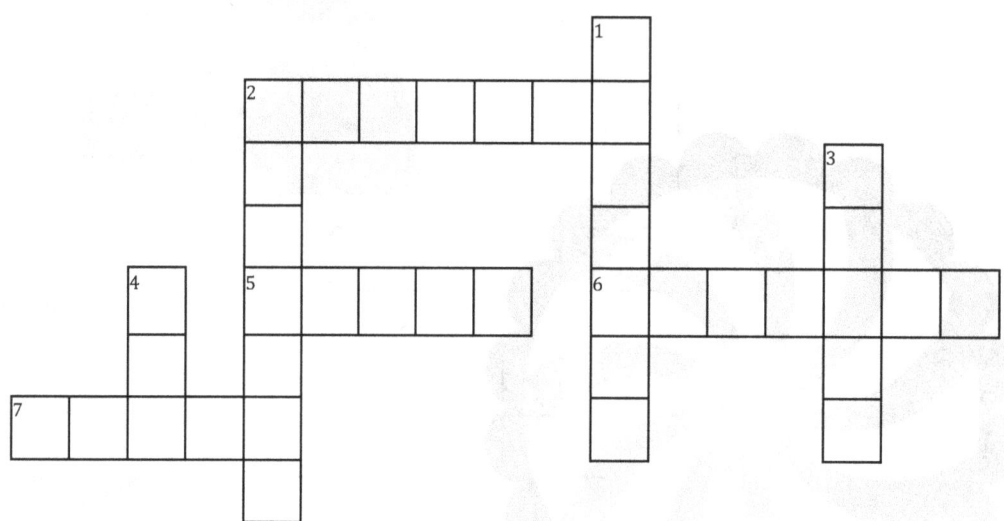

Across

2. Suitcases or trunks used to carry things during travel.

5. A small ship used for private trips or racing.

6. A way of acting that is usual or accepted for a person or a social group.

7. A place with many rooms and beds where people pay money to sleep, eat meals, or buy other services.

Down

1. Something used to carry and move people or things.

2. Suitcases, bags, or trunks used to carry things during travel; luggage.

3. The land beside an ocean, sea, lake, or river.

4. An engine that causes forward movement by the power of a stream of gases being forced out under pressure in the opposite direction. _____ engines are often used in aircraft.

People

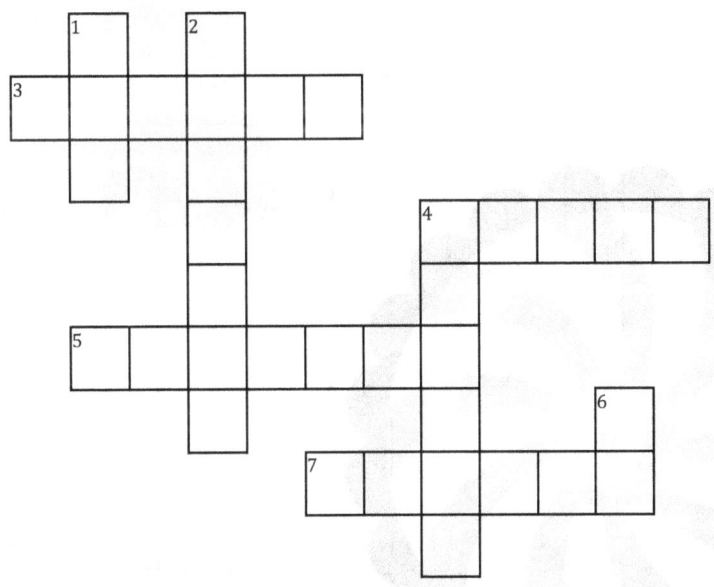

Across

3. A _____ can help you when you're sick or hurt.

4. A _____ is a student, a person who is learning.

5. A _____ is someone who looks after and cleans a building.

7. _____ are human beings.

Down

1. A _____ is a young man.

2. A _____ is a person who is learning.

4. A _____ is a human being.

6. _____ is a word that refers to the person who is speaking or writing.

Body Parts

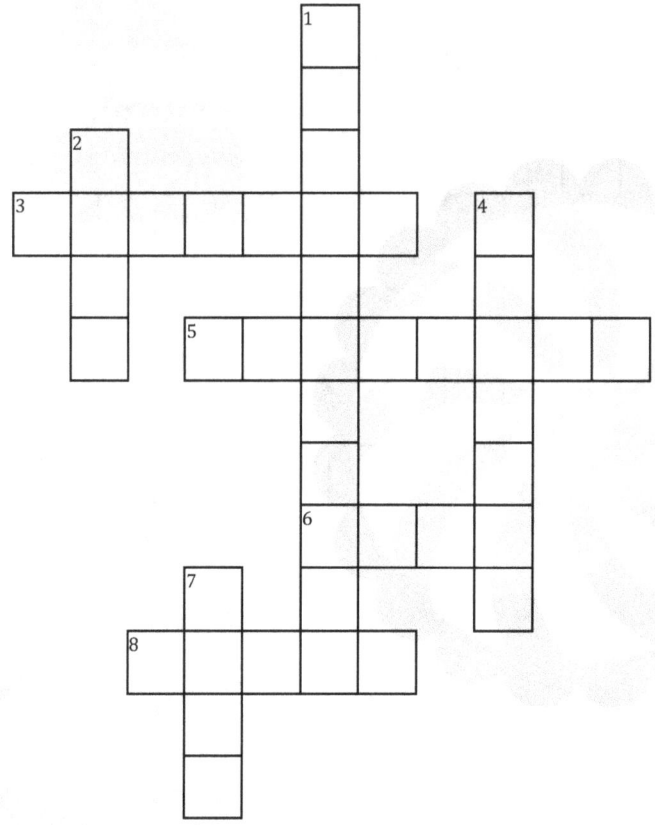

Across

3. It is a clean pad that is used to cover and protect cuts and other injuries.

5. It is the part of the face that is above the eyebrows and below the hair.

6. It is the colored part of the eye around the pupil.

8. We use these to chew food.

Down

1. The pattern marks on our fingertips are _____.

2. These let you open and close your mouth and take bites.

4. These are long hairs on the edges of the eyelids.

7. It is between your head and your shoulders.

Kitchen

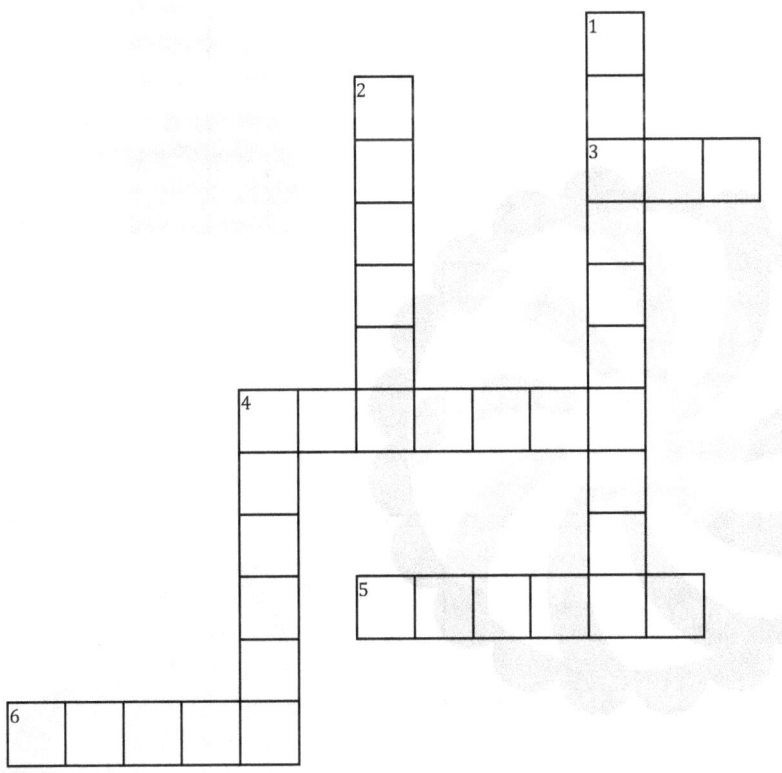

Across

3. A _____ is a dessert that is made with fruit and has a crust.

4. _____s are salty, knotted snacks.

5. The _____ is a soft-bodied marine animal that is protected by two hard shells.

6. A _____ is a dried plum.

Down

1. A _____ is a disposable plate that is made out of paper. People use _____s at picnics.

2. _____s are sweet, juicy fruit.

4. A _____ is a cucumber that is preserved in brine.

Geography

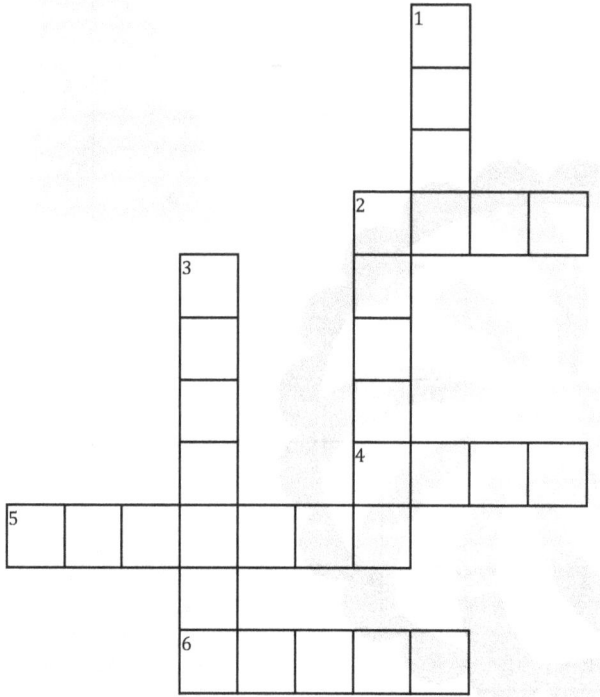

Across

2. Strip, ridge of rocks, sand or coral that rises near the surface of a body of water

4. A large body of fresh or salt water that has land all around it.

5. A deposit of rocks, sand, or clay carried or pushed aside by a moving glacier.

6. Triangular alluvial deposit at the mouth of a river

Down

1. A small hillock formed by wind-blown sand

2. Rough, irregular, loose fragments broken from a large mass of rock

3. Land that is low in respect to the surrounding country.

Weather

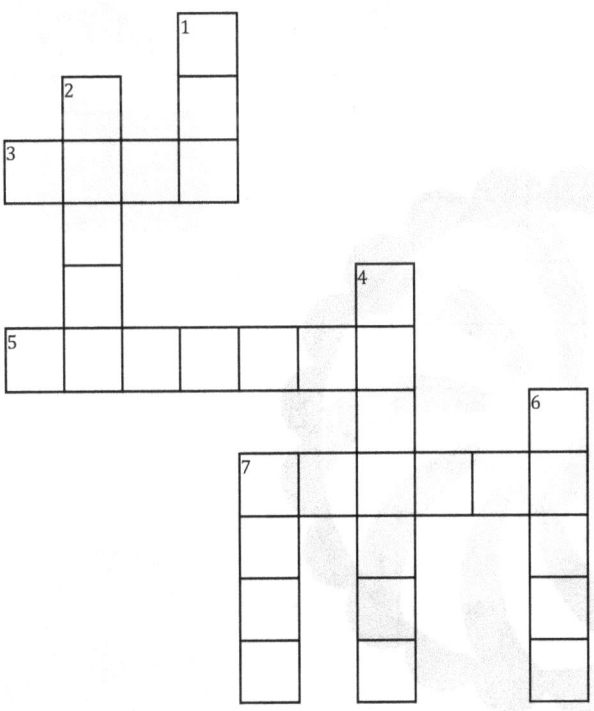

Across

3. Mist, smoke, or dust in the air, making it hard to see.

5. The loud noise you sometimes hear during a violent rain storm.

7. Sudden, violent windstorm accompanied by rain

Down

1. Frozen, solid water.

2. To guard or give close attention to.

4. Prolonged period without rain

6. Snow that is partly melted.

7. A mixture of smoke and fog that is caused by moist air and human pollution.

House

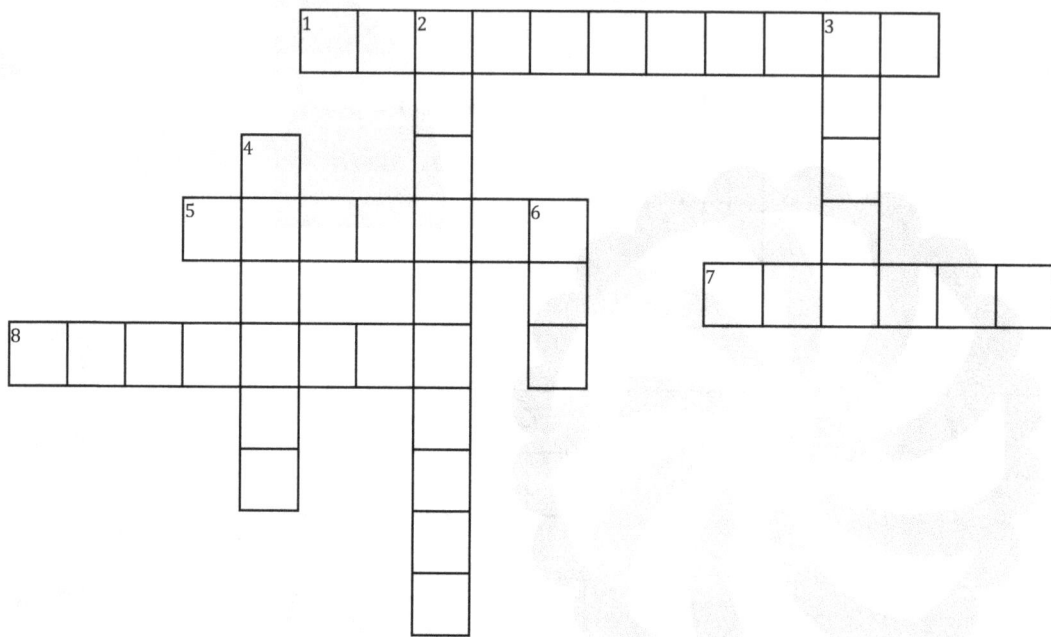

Across

1. A _____ has a mechanical bird that sings every hour.

5. You take a bath in a _____.

7. _____ are cloth hung on and around a window.

8. Books are stored in _____s.

Down

2. _____s are used to hang wet laundry on a clothes line to dry.

3. _____ is well-made pottery that was first made in _____.

4. You can turn water flow on or off at a _____.

6. People sleep in _____s.

Business

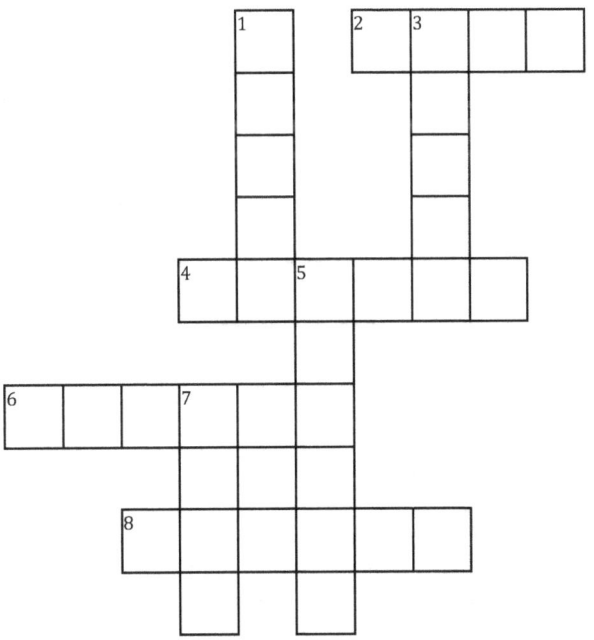

Across

2. To stop doing something.

4. To ask for with force; order.

6. One who sells.

8. The work a person chooses to do through life.

Down

1. A permitted period of vacation or absence.

3. A group of states or countries united under a single government.

5. A place where people buy and sell things.

7. Money or something else that is borrowed or lent.

Season

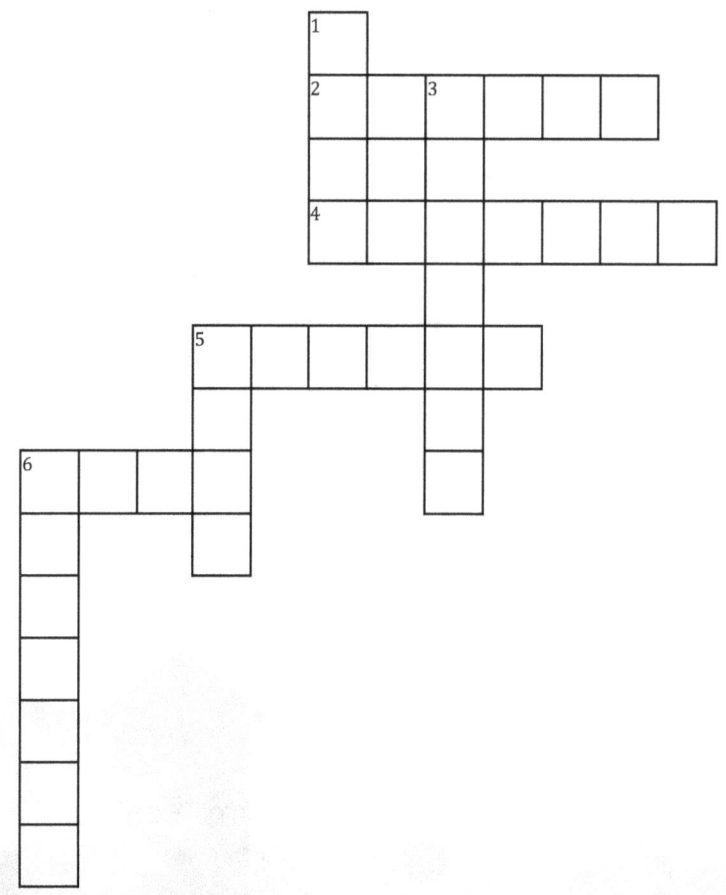

Across

2. _____s are hanging ice that are formed from dripping water.

4. _____ is a game played at Hanukkah.

5. _____s are used to dig. A snow _____ is used to clear away snow.

6. Fly a _____ on a windy day

Down

1. The _____ is air that blows outside.

3. An _____ is a huge chunk of ice that floats in the sea. Most of an _____ is hidden under the water.

5. Plant a _____ and wait for a flower to grow

6. _____ is a holiday that honors African American culture. _____ is celebrated from December until January. The word "_____" means "first fruits" in Swahili.

Animals

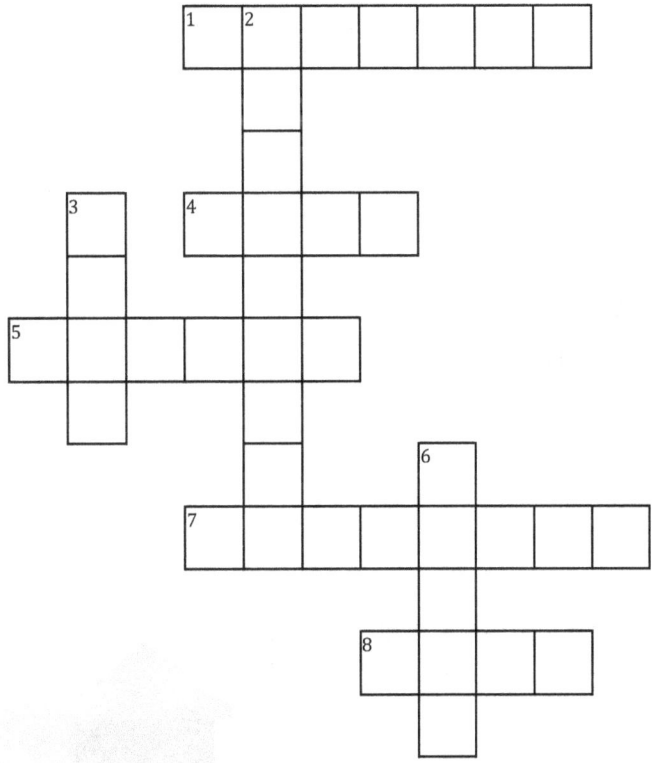

Across

1. A kind of antelope found in Africa and Asia. _____s are mammals with hooves and long legs. They are graceful runners. Their horns are slightly curved and have dark rings.

4. An insect that has four wings and a slender body with a very narrow waist. Some wasps can give a painful sting.

5. A northern sea bird with black and white feathers and a large, flat, colorful bill.

7. An insect with a thin body and two wings. The females bite and suck the blood of animals and people. Some _____es spread disease.

8. An animal with two wings, two feet, and feathers. Most _____s can fly.

Down

2. A mammal whose body is protected by hard, bony plates. _____s live in central and South America, and the Southern United States. Some kinds of _____s are only six inches long; other kinds grow up to four feet in length. They eat mostly insects and are related to sloths and anteaters.

3. The larva of some beetles and other insects. _____s are a young stage in the growth of the insect. They look like short, fat worms.

6. A bird related to the chicken that lives on the ground and is often hunted for sport and food.

School

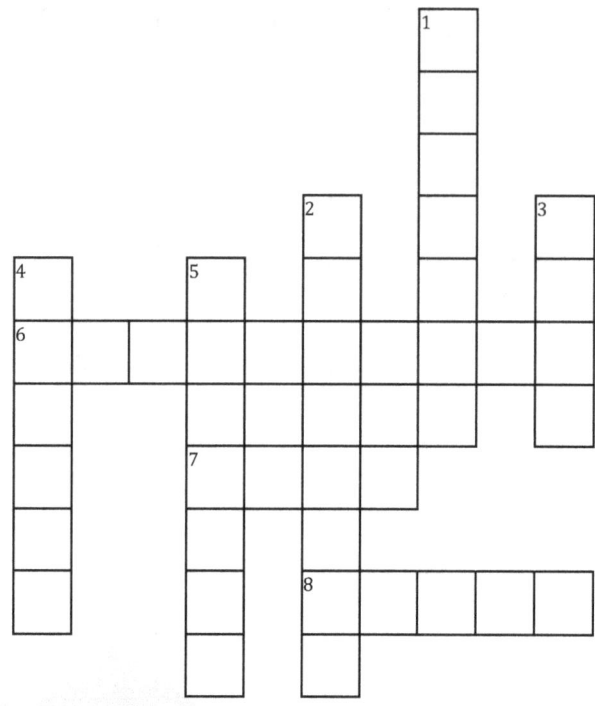

Across

6. To explore by trying different things.

7. A piece of furniture with a flat surface used for writing, using a computer, or reading. _____s usually have drawers where you keep paper, pens, and other supplies.

8. A tool for measuring the length of something. A _____ is marked off in inches, centimeters, or other units.

Down

1. That which separates, divides, or partitions.

2. A tool for cutting paper, fabric, or the like, made up of two blades joined with a pivot so their edges may be opened and closed; _____.

3. A short form of a word that means the study of numbers.

4. A long, thin tool used for writing or drawing. _____s are made of a narrow stick of graphite held within a case of wood.

5. The action or activity of examining and understanding written language.

Vacation

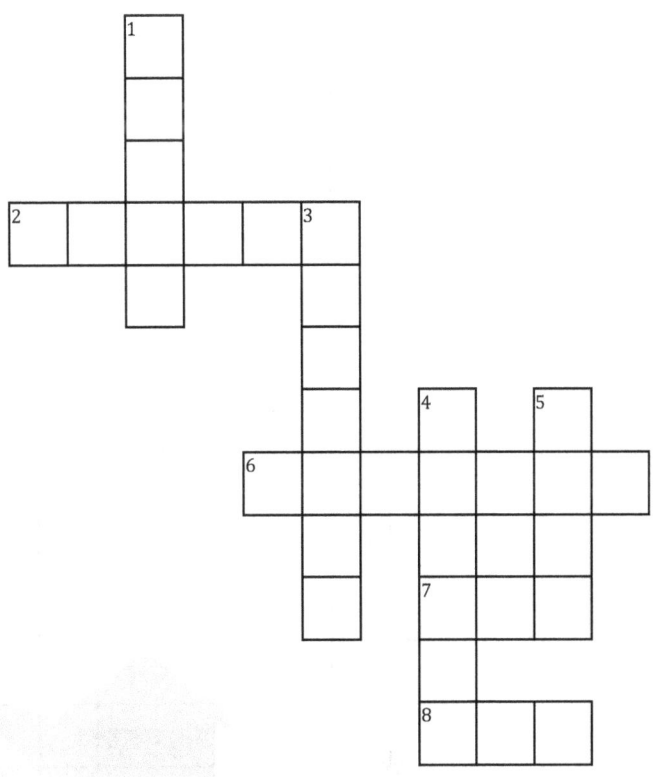

Across

2. A trip on a plane from one place to another.

6. A day on which most people do not work so that they may honor and celebrate some person or event.

7. The top; peak; summit.

8. The salt water covering most of the earth; ocean.

Down

1. A connected series of railroad cars.

3. The act or process, or an instance, of leaving the ground or other surface, as in preparation for flight.

4. A gap or break in activity, time, or space; interruption.

5. An outdoor area where tents or rough shelters are set up to live in or sleep in for a time.

People

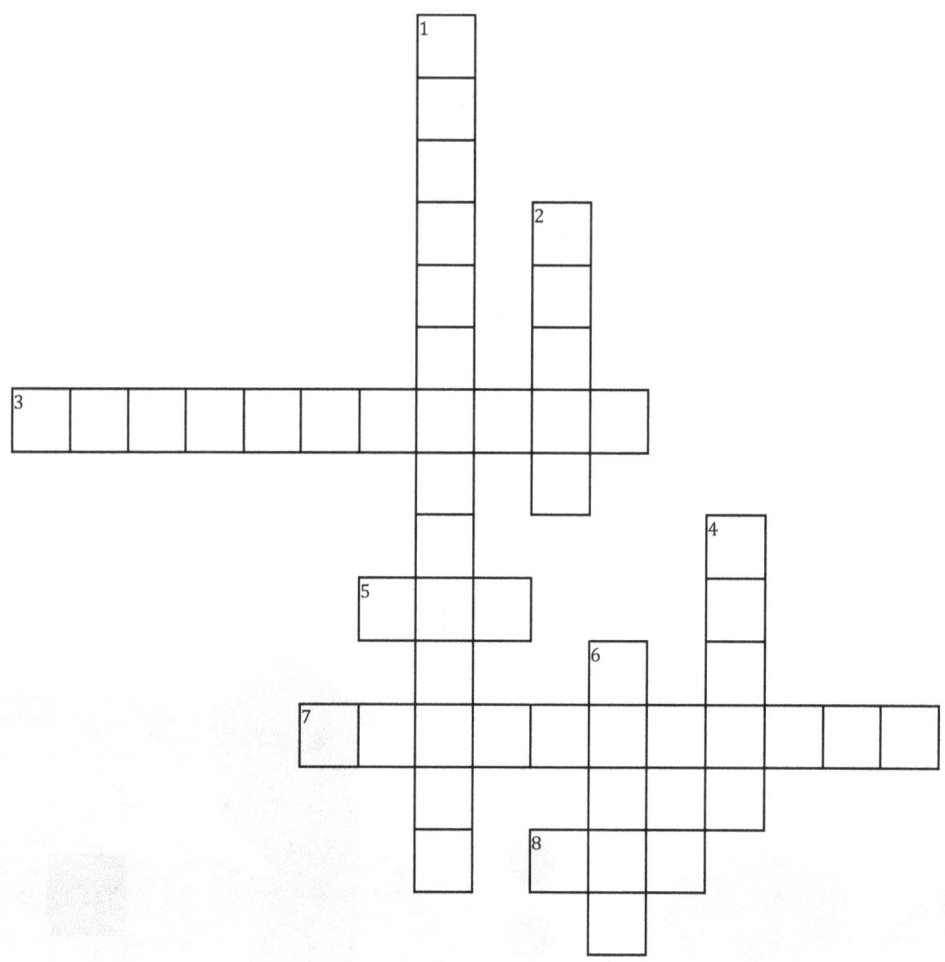

Across

3. The father of your father or mother is your _____.

5. _____ is a word that refers to another person or persons.

7. _____ are five siblings (brothers and/or sisters) who are born at the same time from the same mother.

8. An _____ is a mischievous child.

Down

1. A _____ is a scientist who studies ancient life (like dinosaurs), mostly by looking at fossils.

2. _____s swim under the water.

4. A _____ is a young person.

6. A _____ is a preserved dead body.

Body Parts

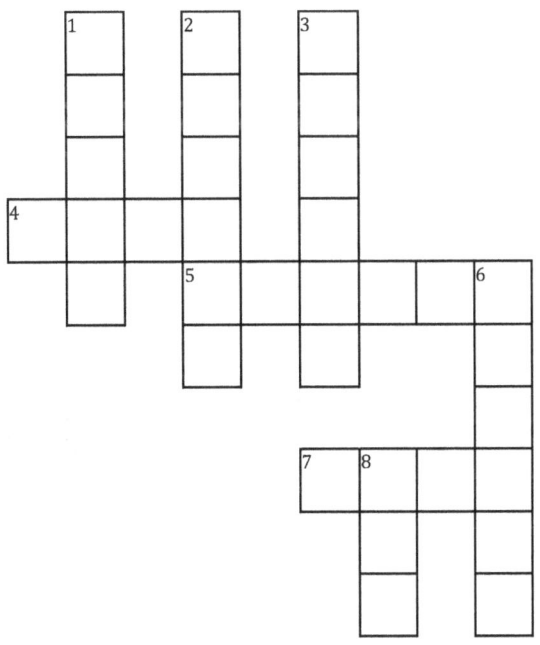

Across

4. Your _____ are below your waist and above your legs.

5. These are flaps of skin that cover and protect our eyes.

7. We have ten toes on our _____.

Down

1. It is the opening in the center of the eye's iris.

2. People have five _____, the _____ of sight, hearing, touch, smell, and taste.

3. We have five these on each hand.

6. They take care of you when you're sick or hurt.

8. We hear things with these.

Kitchen

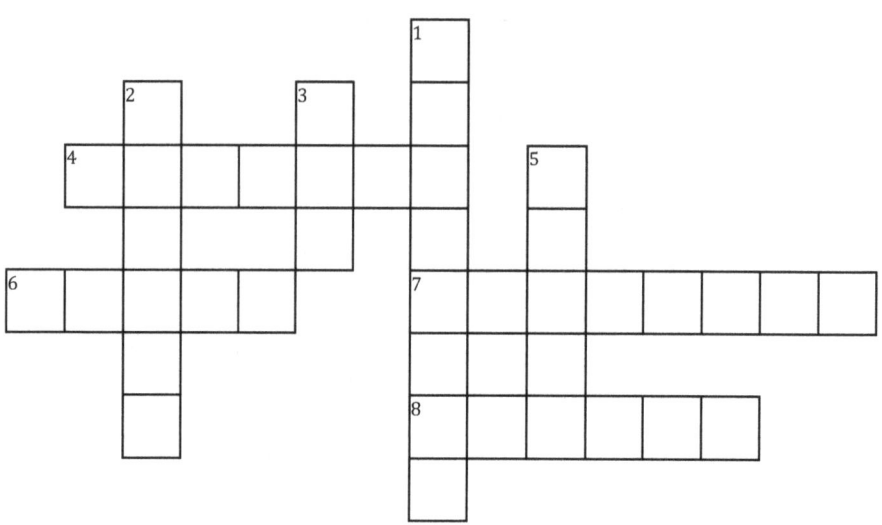

Across

4. _____ is a type of meat.

6. An _____ is an oily fruit that grows on an evergreen tree.

7. _____s are fast-growing fungi. They grow in dark, damp places.

8. You can brew tea in a _____.

Down

1. An _____ protects your hand when you put things in or out of an oven.

2. A _____ is a sharp-tasting vegetable that grows underground.

3. _____ is a spread made from fruit.

5. _____ is a type of food made from flour. Spaghetti and macaroni are types of _____.

Geography

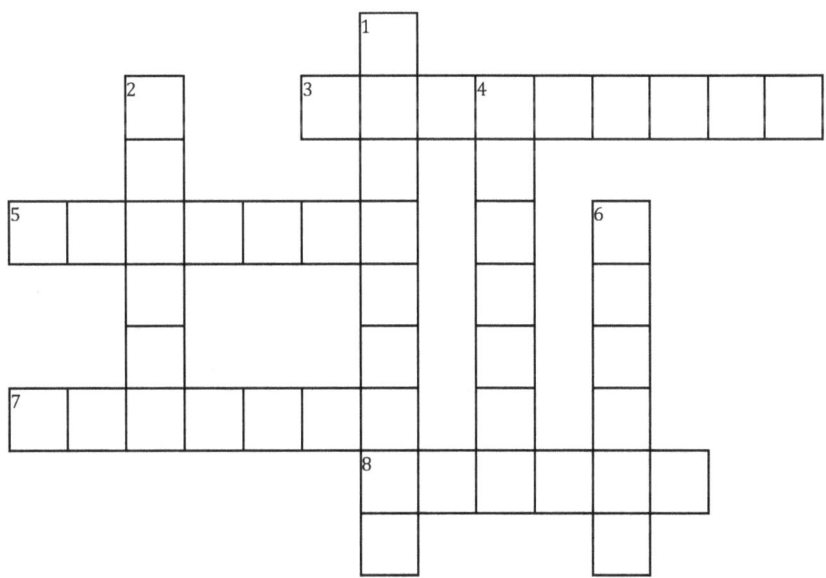

Across

3. Distance on the earth's surface east or west of an imaginary line on the globe that goes from the north pole to the south pole and passes through Greenwich, England. _____ is usually measured in degrees.

5. A way through which something can pass; corridor; channel.

7. Cone shaped mountain that vents hot, molten lava from the earth's interior

8. Not wide.

Down

1. Magnetic rock

2. Skeleton of dead animal or plant preserved in petrified rock form

4. Massive, moving ice layer

6. A shallow body of salt water by the sea. A _____ is separated from the sea by sandbars, coral reefs, or islands.

Weather

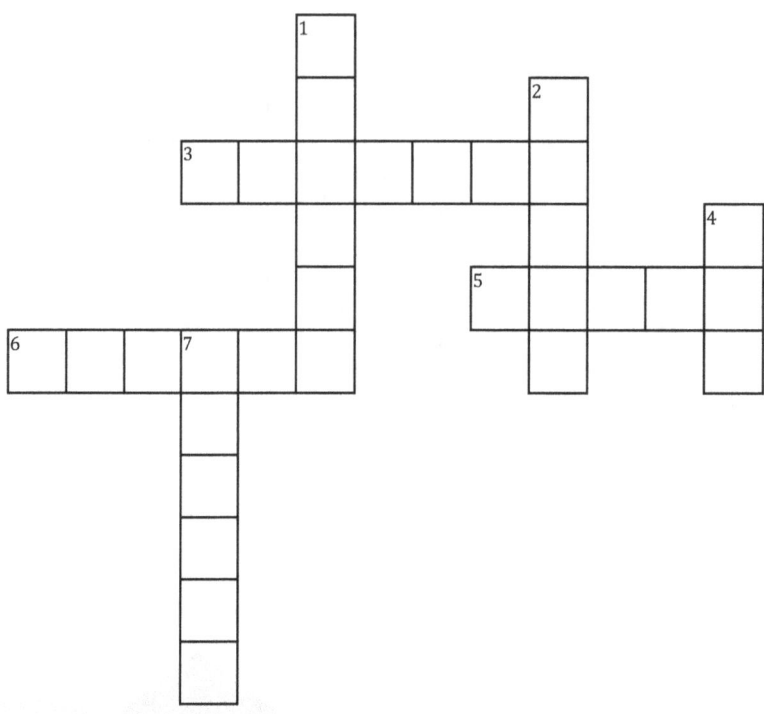

Across

3. A storm of very strong winds that form a cloud shaped like a funnel. Although it does not last long, a _____ destroys everything in its path.

5. Tiny pieces of a liquid or solid that float in a gas.

6. A shining cloud or aura believed to surround a deity that is appearing on earth.

Down

1. Wispy white cloud at high altitude

2. Of or having to do with the north pole or south pole of the earth.

4. Not wet; without any water.

7. A light or gentle wind.

House

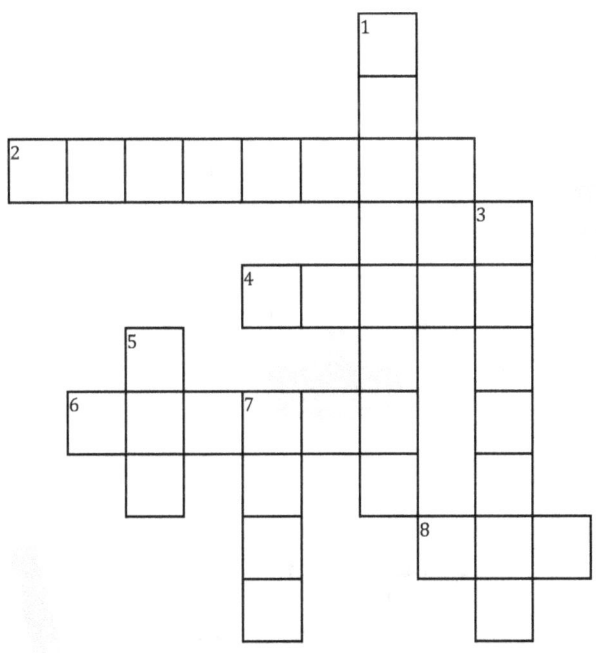

Across

2. Things are stored in _____s.

4. A _____ is a piece of furniture that people sit on.

6. Plants grow in a _____.

8. We use _____s to lock and unlock doors.

Down

1. _____ are cloth hung on and around a window.

3. A _____ keeps things icy.

5. A _____ is a machine that makes a breeze.

7. You can go in and out through a _____.

21

Business

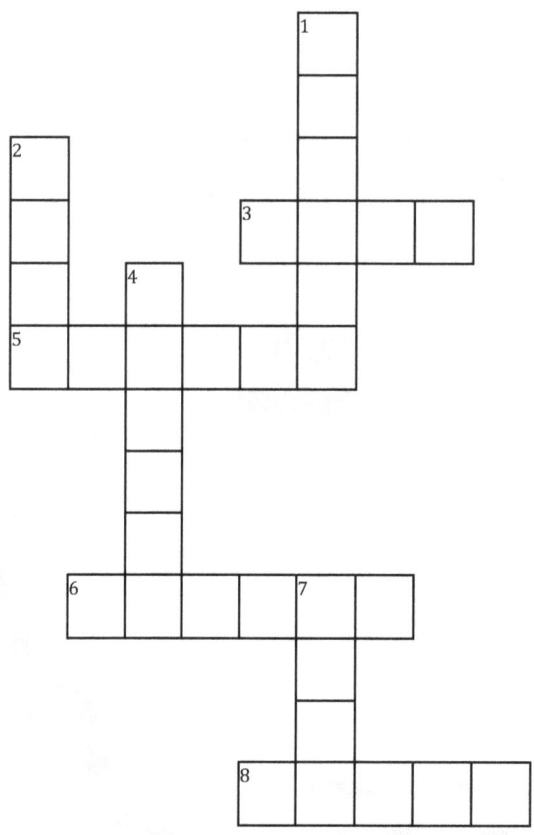

Across

3. An agreement or bargain.

5. The amount of money made by a business that is more than the amount put in at the start.

6. A short written record that tells about a person's education, work experience, and other qualifications for a job.

8. A group of people who manage or direct something.

Down

1. One who pays for the services of another.

2. To place on and send by _____, truck, or other vehicle.

4. The amount of space inside an object or the amount of space that an object uses.

7. A short form of _____randum.

Season

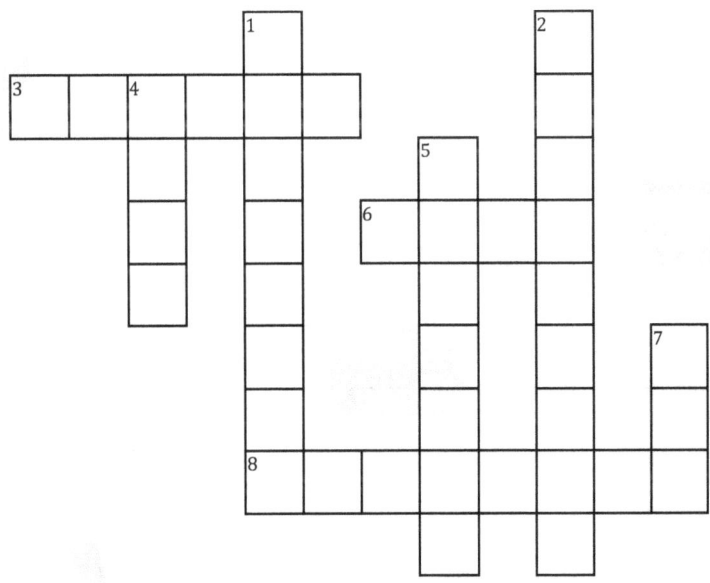

Across

3. You put the eggs that you find into me!

6. A _____ consists of months, weeks, or days.

8. _____ live in the far north.

Down

1. _____ is the twelfth month of the year.

2. An _____ plant doesn't lose its leaves in the winter.

4. _____ is flakes of frozen water that fall from clouds when it is very cold.

5. There are four _____ in the year: winter, spring, summer, and fall (also called autumn).

7. _____ tree is an evergreen tree; it doesn't lose its leaves in the winter.

Animals

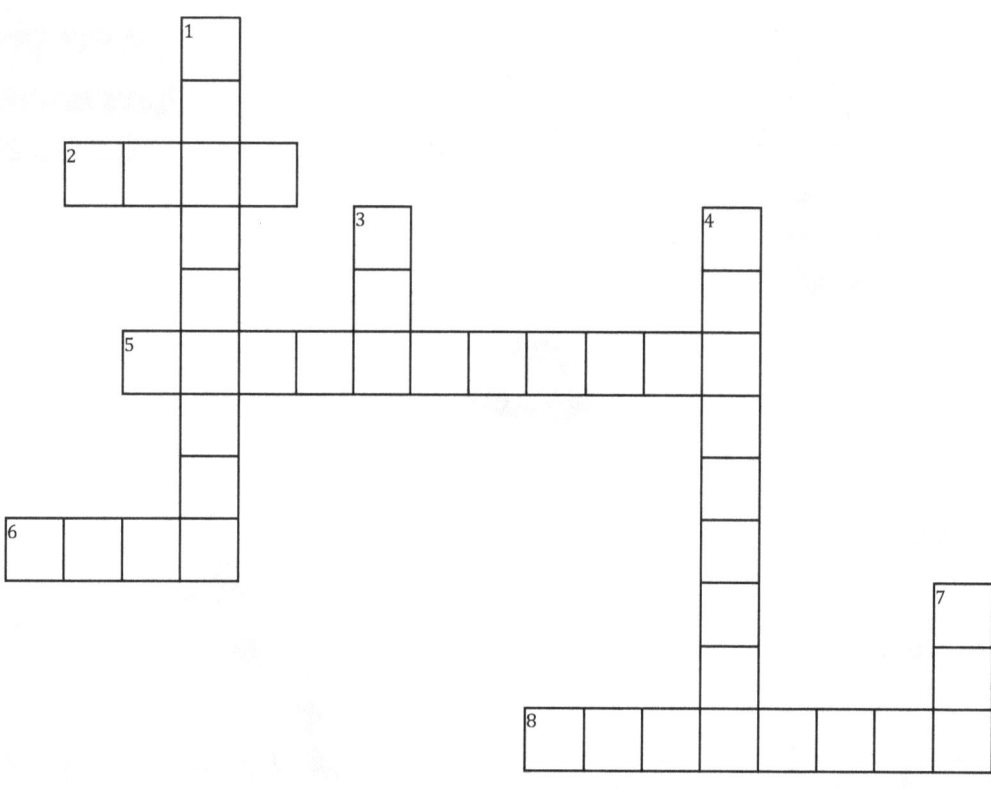

Across

2. A small animal that is related to the spider. _____ attaches themselves to people and other animals and suck their blood. _____ are known to spread disease.

5. The _____, or ratel, is a small mammal that is very strong and tough. It is a member of the weasel family, which includes skunks.

6. A flying insect with four large wings. Most _____ wings have dull colors.

8. _____ rabbit is a small mammal that lives in South Africa. It is one of the most endangered animals in the world.

Down

1. An insect with a flat body and long antennae that lives in most parts of the world. Some kinds of _____es are pests that live in homes and other buildings. All _____es are active at night.

3. A small common insect with two wings. Sometimes flies carry disease.

4. A small mammal with bristles or spines in its fur. _____s are rodents closely related to guinea pigs, but much larger. Some _____s have quills with barbs that hurt any animal that attacks them. Different kinds of _____s live in north and south America, Europe, Africa, and Asia.

7. A black and yellow insect that sometimes stings. Some kinds of _____s make honey from flowers.

24

School

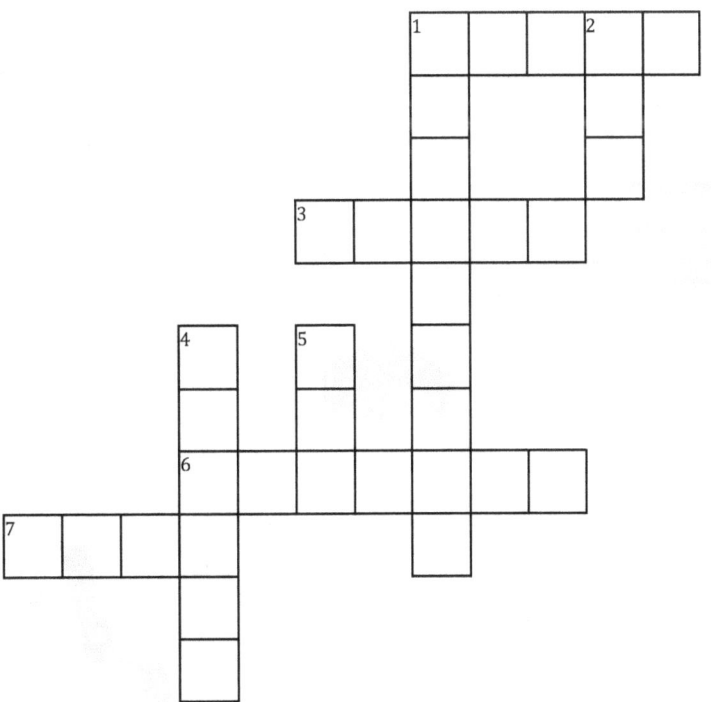

Across

1. A person who is taught by a teacher.

3. A meal eaten in the middle of the day, or any light meal during the day.

6. An instrument for showing direction. A typical _____ has a moving magnetic needle that points north.

7. A long narrow strip of plastic, cloth, or paper that has glue on one side. _____ is used to stick things together.

Down

1. The person who is head of a school.

2. A colored liquid in pens.

4. A relaxing break from an activity, such as school classes or trials in court.

5. A short form of _____nasium.

Vacation

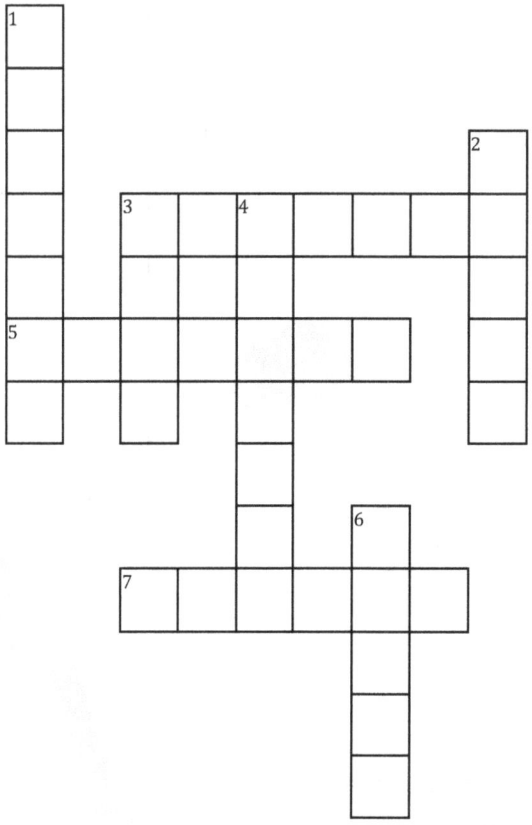

Across

3. A way through which something can go; corridor; channel.

5. Fare for traveling by aircraft, especially by airplane.

7. To move about with no purpose, aim, or plan; roam.

Down

1. A major public road on which one can drive at high speeds, especially between cities.

2. To go away from or depart.

3. A place where ships load and unload, and its nearby town or city.

4. The place where a person or thing is normally found.

6. The land at the edge of a lake, ocean, or other body of water. A beach slopes gently toward the water and usually has sand or pebbles.

People

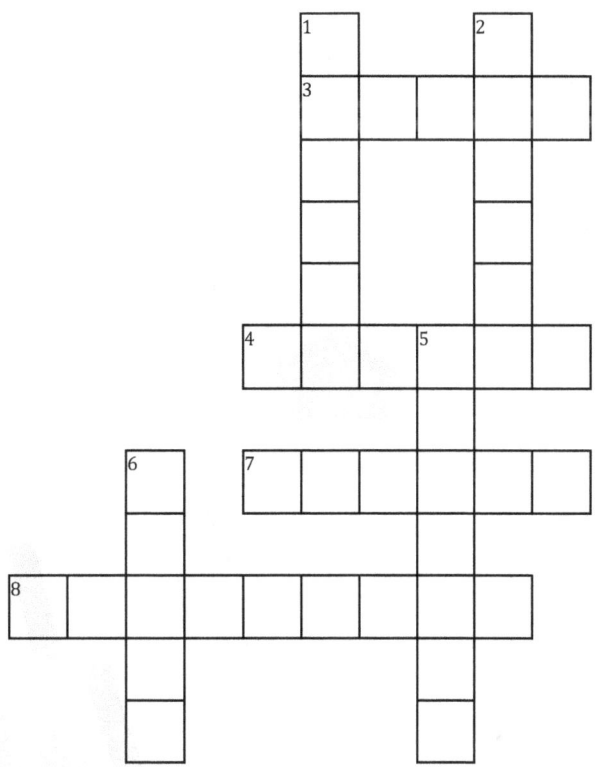

Across

3. An _____ is someone who performs a role in a play or a movie.

4. An _____ shoots an arrow with a bow.

7. A _____ is a group of related people.

8. A _____ is a young person.

Down

1. A _____ is a man who has a child.

2. The _____ enforce laws and keep order.

5. An _____ is a girl or woman who has inherited or will inherit a lot of money.

6. _____ divers swim under the water and carry their own air in a tank on their back.

Body Parts

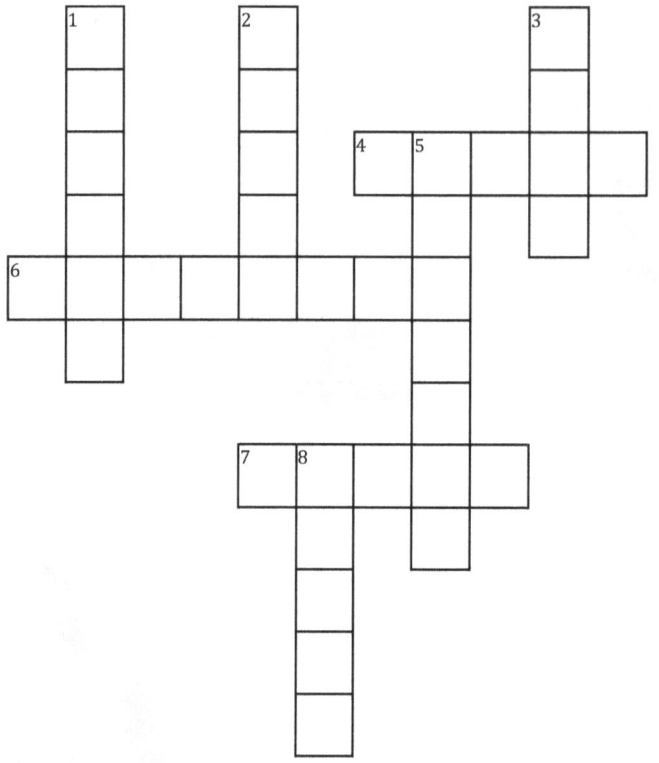

Across

4. It is the middle of the body, between the chest and the hips.

6. It is one of the series of small, connected bones in the spine that surround and protect the spinal cord.

7. It is the widest finger on a person's hand. It is next to the pointing finger. All apes (like gorillas and chimps) have these.

Down

1. These are bean-shaped organs that take waste from the blood and produce urine.

2. It is the joint between your foot and leg.

3. We use this to breathe; it also gives us a sense of smell.

5. It is a science that studies the body.

8. It pumps blood throughout your body.

Kitchen

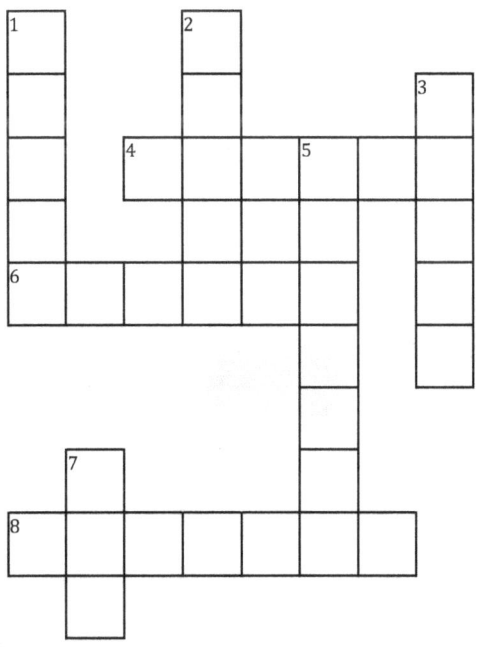

Across

4. _____s are small, baked goods made from a batter.

6. A _____ is a pot in which you boil water.

8. _____is a snack food made from corn that bursts open after being heated.

Down

1. A _____ is used to beat eggs or batter.

2. _____ is the part of some plants that contains the seeds. Apples, strawberries, oranges, and bananas are _____.

3. You can cut things with a _____.

5. A _____ keeps things icy.

7. A _____ is a cooking pot used in asia.

Geography

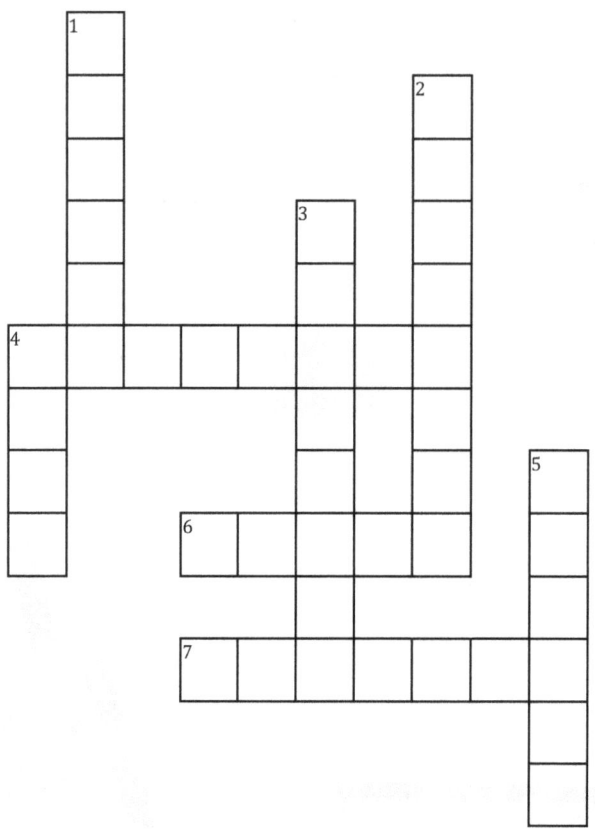

Across

4. Material deposited by water or wind

6. A large, flat area of land without trees.

7. Low grade brown coal

Down

1. A small stone that has become smooth through erosion

2. A land mass with great height and steep sides. It is much higher than a hill.

3. To extend out over.

4. Loose sedimentary material consisting of very fine particles

5. A large roofed-over cave in a rock

Weather

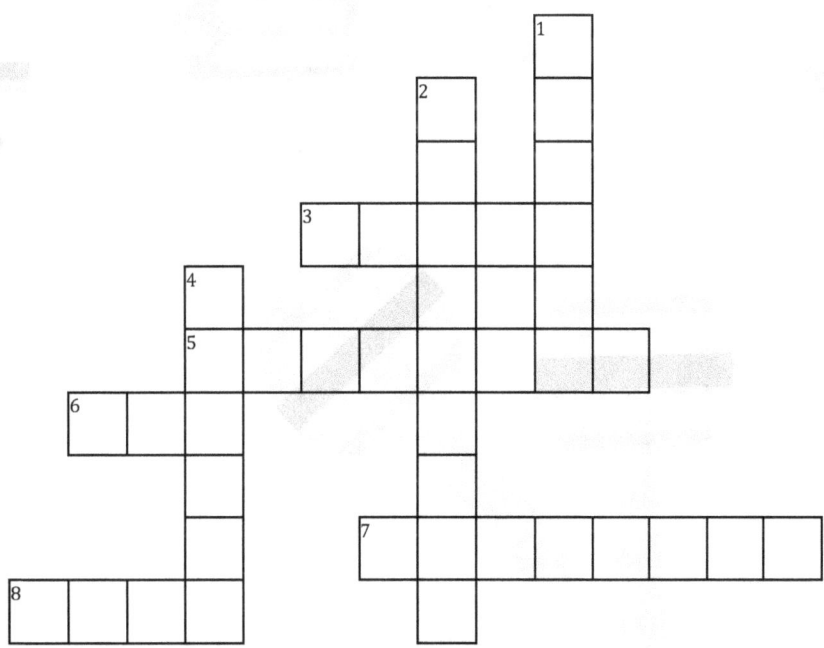

Across

3. Frozen or partly frozen rain

5. A steady force upon a surface.

6. Moisture condensed at night on surfaces of cool objects

7. In the direction that the wind is going; leeward.

8. Low temperature in the environment.

Down

1. The season of the year between autumn and spring.

2. Powerful, turbulent whirlpool

4. In or toward the direction from which the wind is blowing.

House

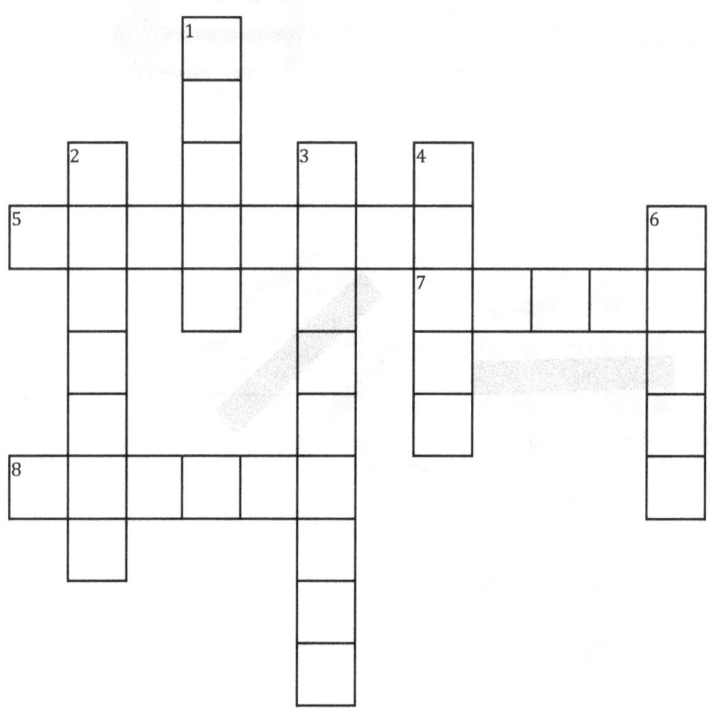

Across

5. An _____ is a chair with arms.

7. An _____ is a house made out of blocks of ice. Brr!

8. A _____ is a pot in which you boil water.

Down

1. A few people can sit on a _____.

2. A _____ is a piece of furniture in which you can store things.

3. A _____ is a device that opens cans.

4. This fireplace is made out of _____s.

6. A _____ is a big, soft piece of furniture that many people can sit on.

Business

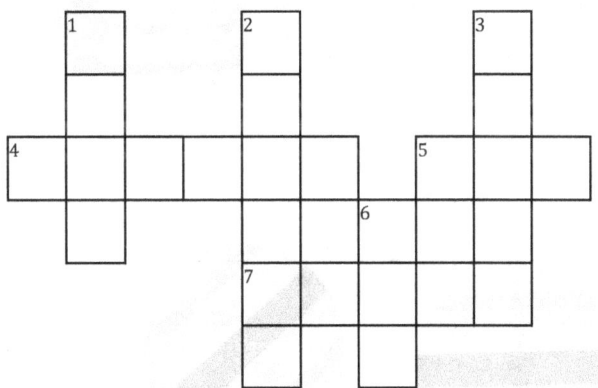

Across

4. A small, printed piece of paper. A _____ gives a person a lower price on something.

5. A machine for sending and receiving pages over telephone lines to or from another machine of this kind.

7. The act of buying and selling things, especially things that are produced in one country and sold to customers in another country.

Down

1. A small store.

2. The process of growing.

3. An agreement to pay to use another person's property for a certain period of time.

6. Money that you pay to a government. The government uses the money to provide services.

Season

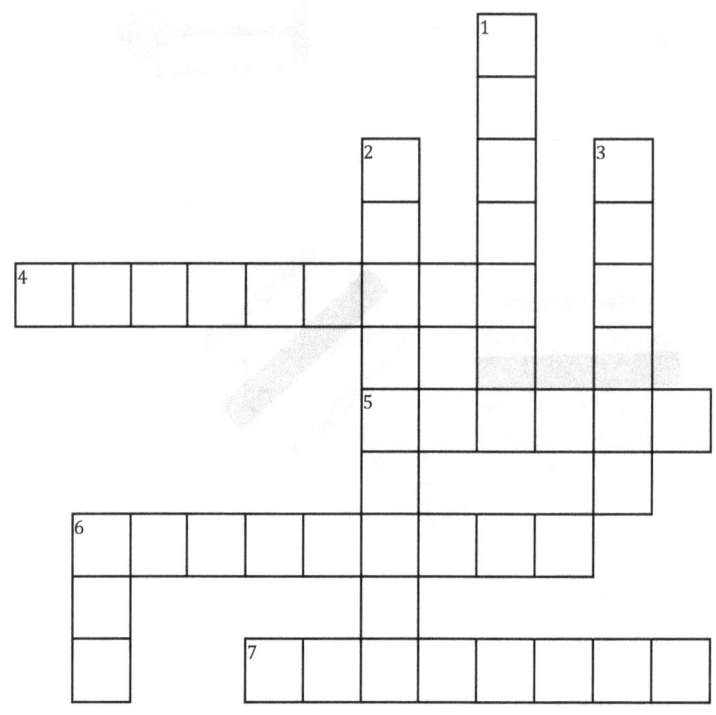

Across

4. The _____ is the northernmost place on earth. There is no land at the _____, but there is a layer of ice on top of the arctic ocean around the pole.

5. A place to plant flowers or plants

6. A yellow flower that faces the sun

7. An _____ will keep you warm when it is cold.

Down

1. The beginning of a year is called the _____. People often celebrate on this day. A year consists of months, weeks, or days.

2. The _____ is a migratory bird from north America.

3. _____s keep your hands warm.

6. When you _____, you glide over snow or water.

Animals

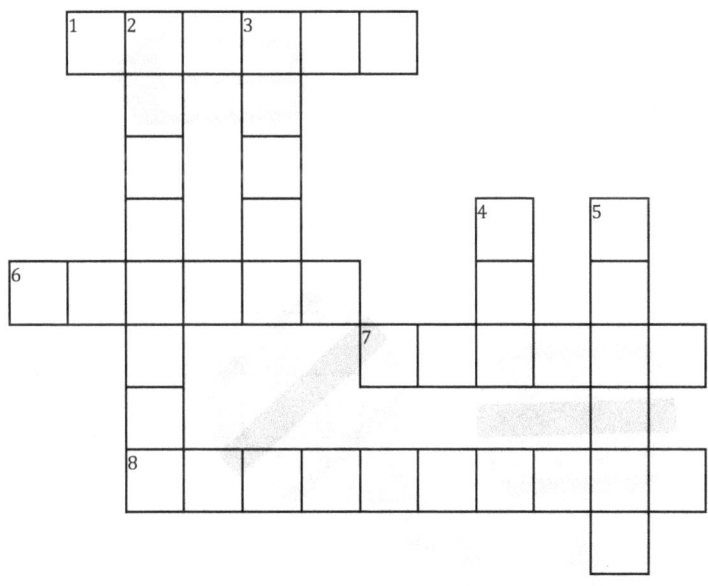

Across

1. A furry mammal with short legs and a long body. The American _____ has a white stripe on its forehead that runs down its back, and it has long dark marks on its face also. _____s eat worms, rodents, rabbits, and plants. Different kinds of _____s live in Europe, Asia, and North America. They are related to skunks, otters, and other kinds of weasels.

6. _____s are meat-eating mammals that are excellent hunters. They are closely related to mink, ferrets, and wolverines.

7. A small, intelligent mammal in the same family as humans. _____s live in places with a warm climate.

8. A large mammal with hooves and very thick skin. _____es have one or two horns on their noses. They eat plants. Wild _____es live in Africa and Southern Asia. Four of the five kinds of _____es are in danger of becoming extinct.

Down

2. A mammal that uses its long, sticky tongue to eat ants and termites. True _____s have no teeth, are furry, and live in central or south America. They are related to armadillos and sloths. Other kinds of mammals that eat ants are also sometimes called _____s, but they are not related to American _____s.

3. A bird with a long neck and large feet that lives in or near water. People hunt or keep geese for their meat.

4. An adult female bird. People keep chicken _____s for their eggs and meat.

5. A wild cat with yellow or brown fur and black spots or stripes. _____s look like leopards but are smaller. They live in south and central America, sometimes as far north as Texas. They are carnivorous mammals that eat birds, snakes, and small mammals.

School

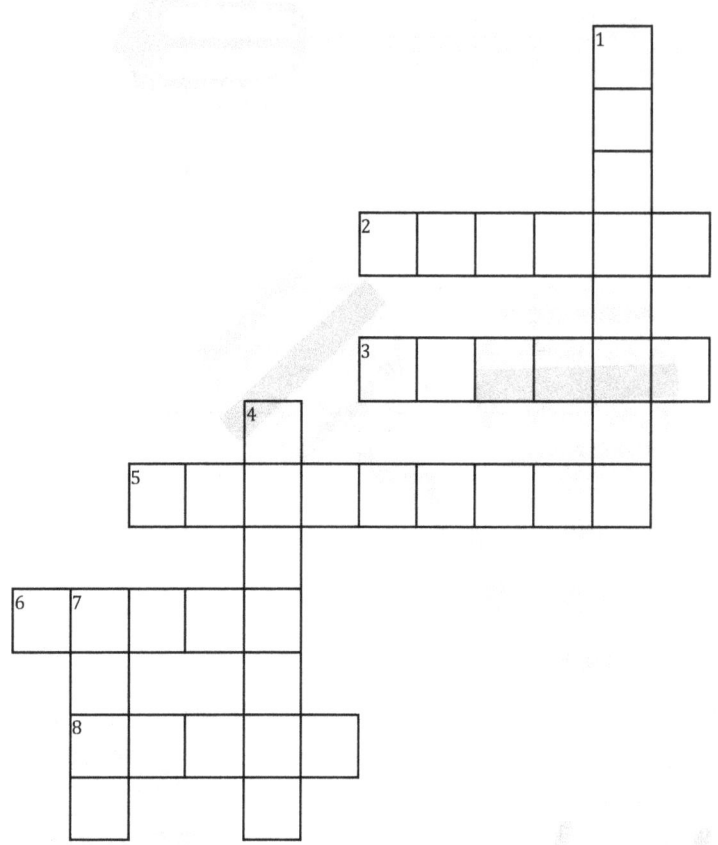

Across

2. A large, sturdy notebook cover that contains a device for holding loose papers.

3. A place for teaching and learning.

5. A measuring stick three feet long.

6. Clever; intelligent.

8. To use the power of the mind.

Down

1. A book of blank pages to keep notes in.

4. The letters or words written by someone.

7. A short form of a word that means the study of numbers, amounts, shapes, and the relationship between them.

Vacation

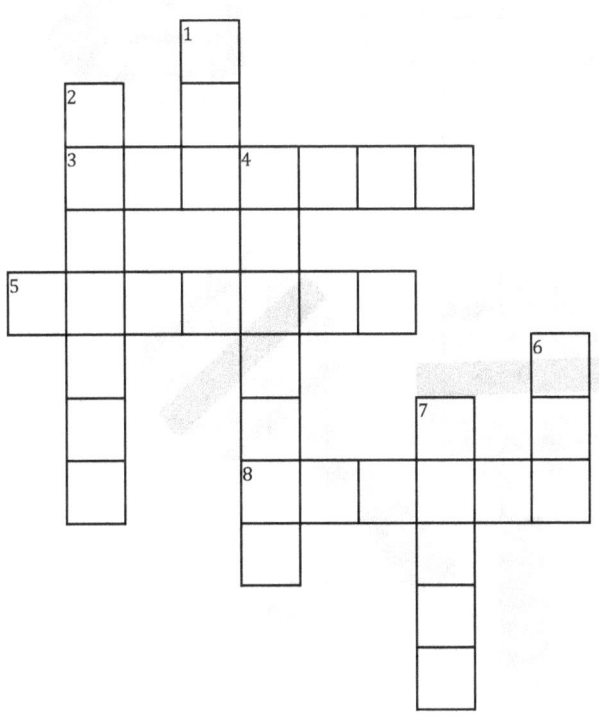

Across

3. To travel across or through in order to discover or search for something.

5. Arrival upon the ground or other surface.

8. To go back or come back.

Down

1. A picture of a particular area of the earth or sky drawn or printed to scale on a flat surface.

2. A place where one escapes for relaxation.

4. Freedom from work or other duties that take time and effort; free time.

6. A small hotel for people who are travelling.

7. To direct or lead along a way that is not familiar.

People

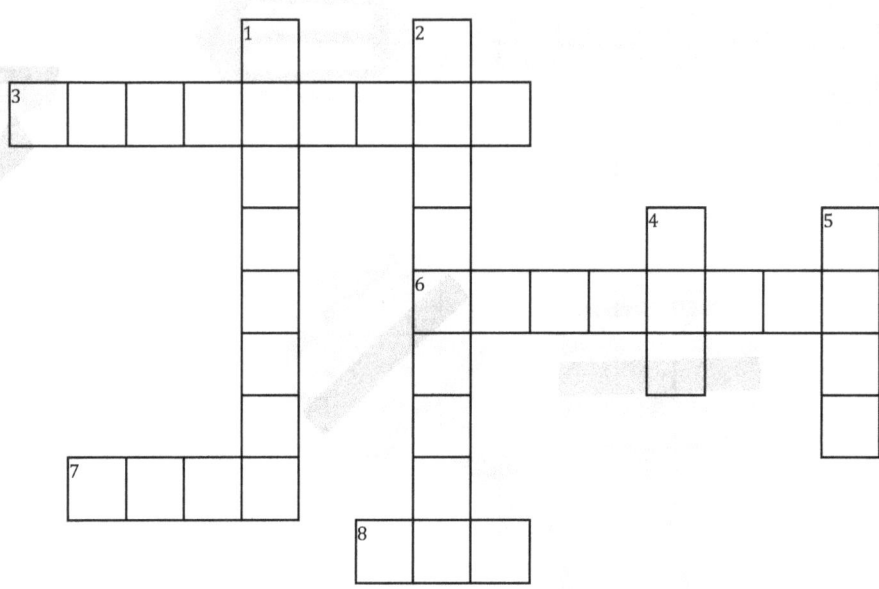

Across

3. _____s take care of libraries and help people find books.

6. An _____ explores unknown places and discovers new things. For example, Magellan was an _____ who led the first expedition that sailed around the earth.

7. An _____ is a person who has inherited or will inherit something of value.

8. _____ is another word for father.

Down

1. A _____ is a female offspring.

2. A _____ is a woman who does ballet dancing.

4. A _____ is a male offspring.

5. An _____ is a unified group of people who are trained to fight on land.

Body Parts

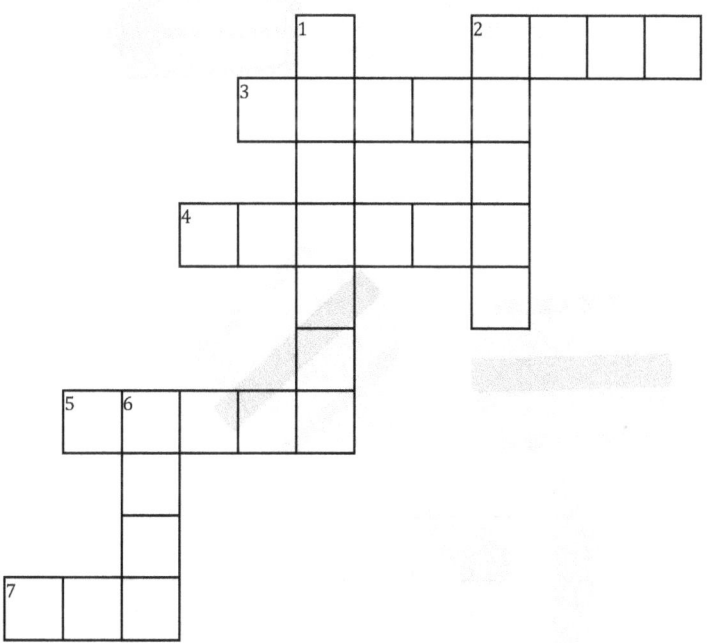

Across

2. It is the part of the face below the mouth.

3. We use it to eat and talk.

4. It has taste buds and helps us eat, taste, and talk.

5. It is the bony structure of head that encloses the brain and supports the jaws.

7. These give us a sense of sight.

Down

1. It grows at the ends of your toes.

2. These are the sides of the face between the mouth area and the ear.

6. It is where the leg bends. It is between the lower leg and the upper leg.

Kitchen

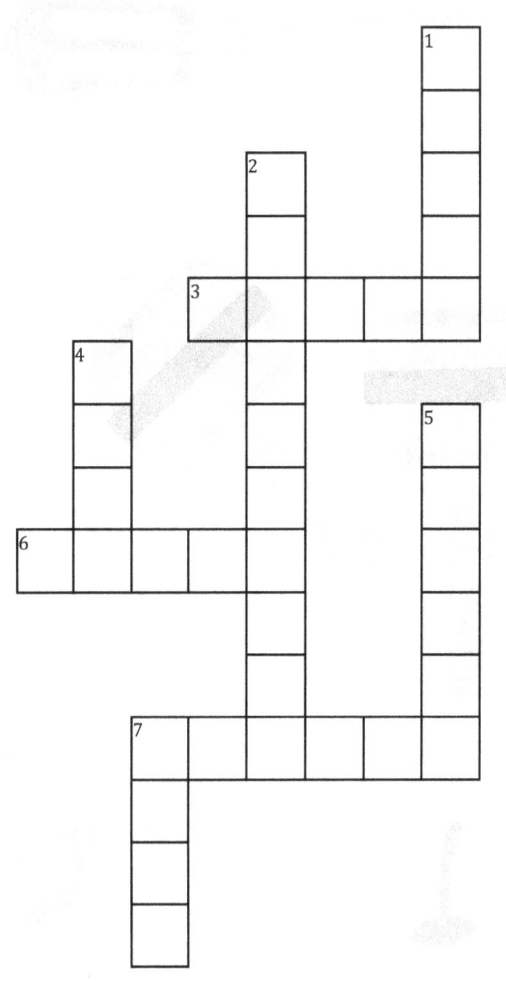

Across

3. A _____ is a large spoon used to serve soup and gravy.

6. _____ is a liquid that we drink and use to wash. _____ covers over two thirds of the surface of the earth, and much of our body is made of _____.

7. _____es are starchy vegetables that grow underground.

Down

1. _____ is pressed from fruit or vegetables.

2. _____s are a type of citrus fruit that sometime squirt you when you eat them.

4. The _____ is a very large, bony fish that lives in the ocean. People eat a lot of _____.

5. _____es are soft and tangy; they grow on vines.

7. A _____ is a sweet, juicy, purple fruit.

Geography

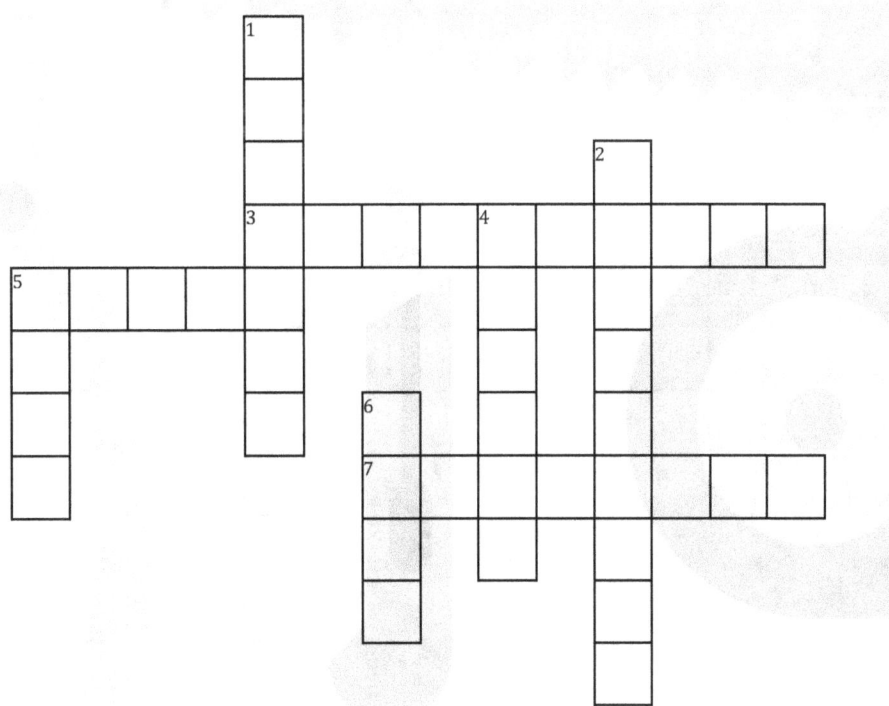

Across

3. The shape of the earth's surface across an area or region. The _____ of an area includes the size and location of hills and dips in the land.

5. A long, narrow, raised section at the top of something; crest.

7. To allow a view over.

Down

1. Flat, broad area of at least ft. Above sea level

2. A level, elevated expanse of land; plateau.

4. A natural hot spring that intermittently ejects a column of water and stream into the air

5. A small brook or creek.

6. Rich soil of clay, sand and organic matter

Weather

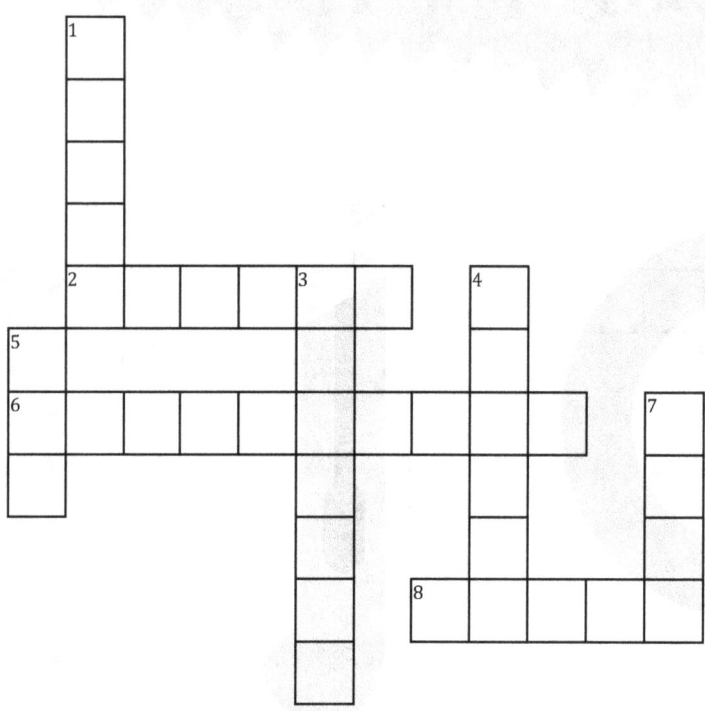

Across

2. Heavy rain fall causing a flood

6. To cover or overspread with water, esp. a very large amount; flood.

8. To be carried away by wind or water.

Down

1. Having a high amount of water in the air.

3. Precipitation in the form of snow pellets.

4. A line on a weather map drawn between places that have the same barometric pressure during a given time or period.

5. The mixture of gases that is in the space around the earth. People need _____ to live.

7. A mass or cloud of tiny water drops in the air.

House

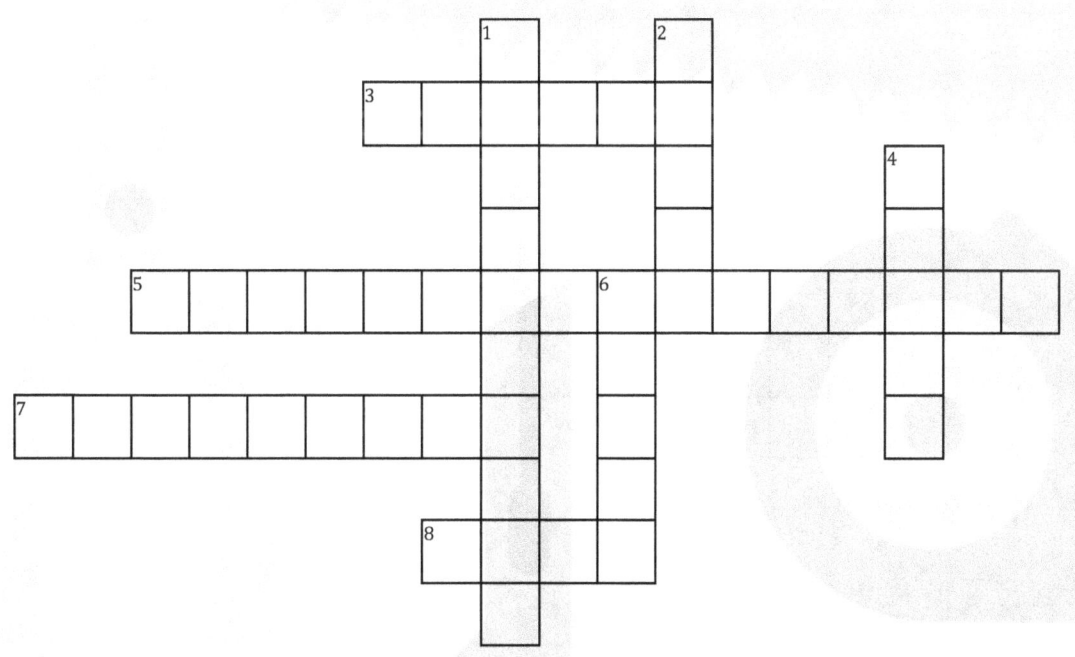

Across

3. A _____ is a small bed for a baby.

5. A _____ is a large, free-standing pendulum clock.

7. Tables, chairs, sofas, and beds are _____.

8. A _____ is a door in a fence.

Down

1. _____s hold garbage.

2. A _____ is a type of barrier.

4. You can sweep the floor with a _____.

6. Some people live in _____s.

Business

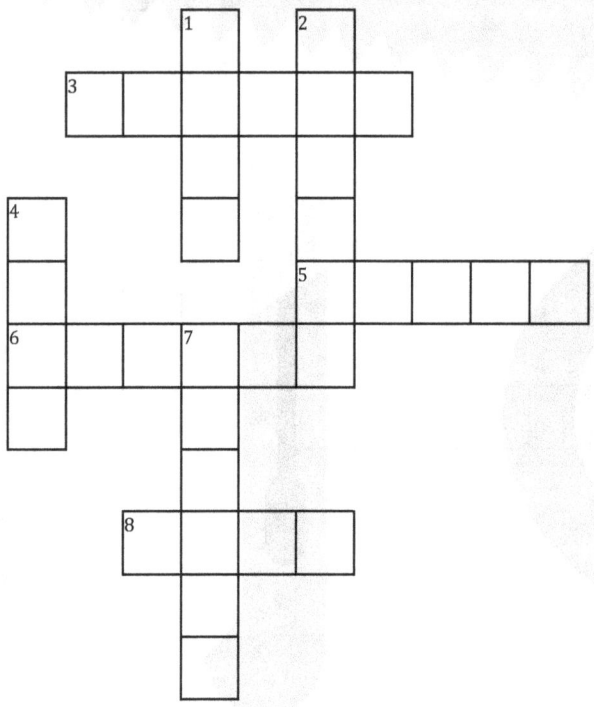

Across

3. The act or process of sending information from a smaller computer to a larger computer or computer network.

5. Things to buy and sell.

6. A formal statement that you intend to end a job or arrangement.

8. A piece of paper that a government or business gives when it borrows money. A _____ promises to repay the sum of money along with interest.

Down

1. An action one intends to take; aim.

2. To direct or control.

4. A position as compared to other positions.

7. Money you get from work that you do or property that you own.

Season

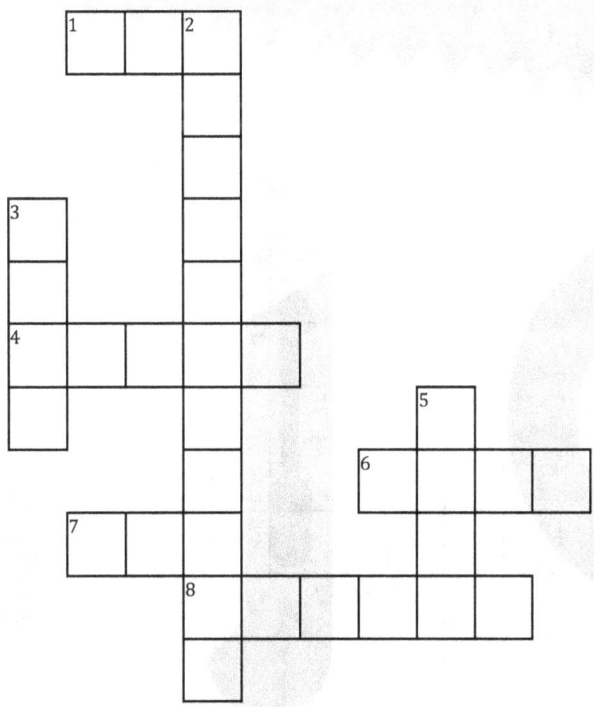

Across

1. A _____ is a short piece of a tree trunk.

4. A _____ is very bad weather, like a blizzard or a thunder_____.

6. March rolls in like a lion, out like a ____

7. When you wear skates, you can glide across _____.

8. _____ is the season between summer and winter. Another name for _____ is fall.

Down

2. _____ is a spicy cookie. _____ men and _____ women are cookies shaped like little people.

3. Birds make a _____ to lay eggs

5. Temperature that is not too cold and not too hot

45

Animals

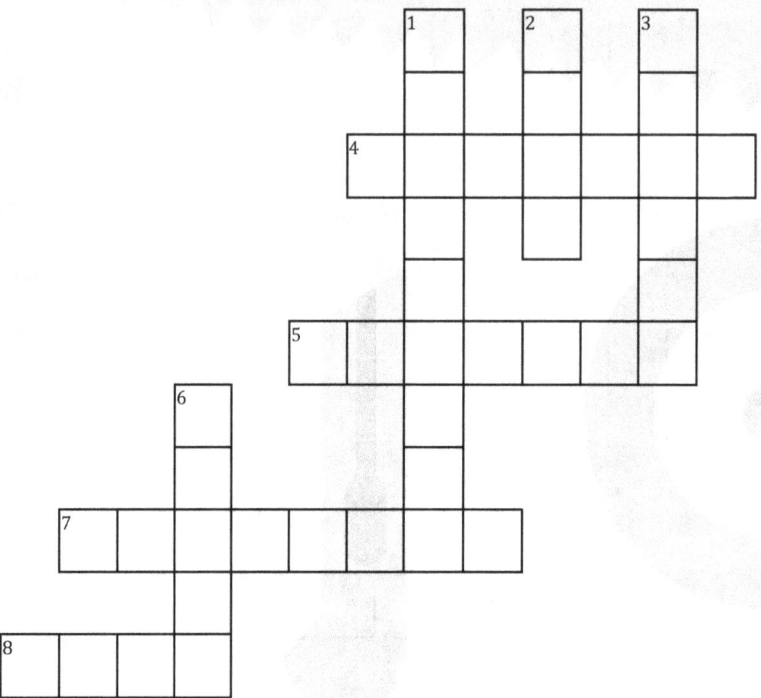

Across

4. Any of various marsupials native to Australia and strongly resembling small or medium-sized kangaroos.

5. An insect that is related to a grasshopper. It has long antennae and strong hind legs for jumping. The male makes a chirping noise by rubbing his front wings together.

7. _____s are the largest living land animals. There are three species, or kinds: the African Savanna _____, the African forest _____, and the Asian _____.

8. A large edible freshwater fish, found or bred in lakes and ponds.

Down

1. Any of a variety of grouse that are found in cold, northern regions, and whose brown plumage is replaced by white in the winter.

2. A wild mammal that is related to the dog and often travels with its group to hunt other animals.

3. A small mammal with soft fur, long ears, long back legs, and a short tail.

6. _____ are among the most valuable of all domestic animals. Domestic animals are ones that have been tamed for use by humans. People eat _____ meat and drink _____ milk.

School

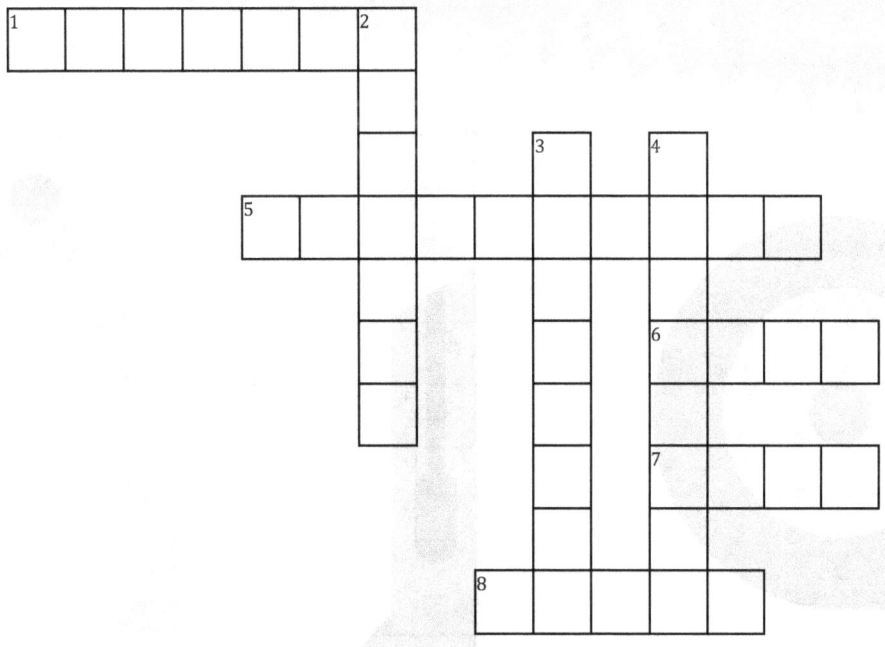

Across

1. A person who goes to a school or college.

5. A book, or a source of information found on a computer, that lists the words of a language in alphabetical order, along with information about their meaning, spelling, and pronunciation.

6. A short form of a word that means a test given at school or a physical checkup.

7. A piece of furniture with drawers and a flat surface used for reading and writing.

8. To get knowledge about something through study or experience.

Down

2. One whose job is teaching; instructor.

3. A set of shelves for holding books.

4. A chart of the days, weeks, and months of one or more years.

Vacation

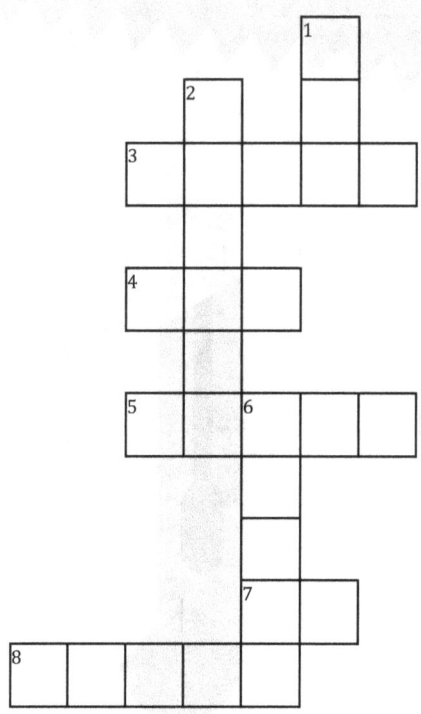

Across

3. The land next to the ocean; seashore.

4. An automobile.

5. To rest while doing nothing or by spending time doing enjoyable things.

7. To move; travel.

8. To travel in a car, truck or other private motor vehicle.

Down

1. A long motor vehicle with many rows of seats used to carry large numbers of people. _____es usually travel along a regular route.

2. A long journey by air, land, sea, or outer space.

6. A cabin, hut, or other shelter meant to be used by people doing outdoor activities.

People

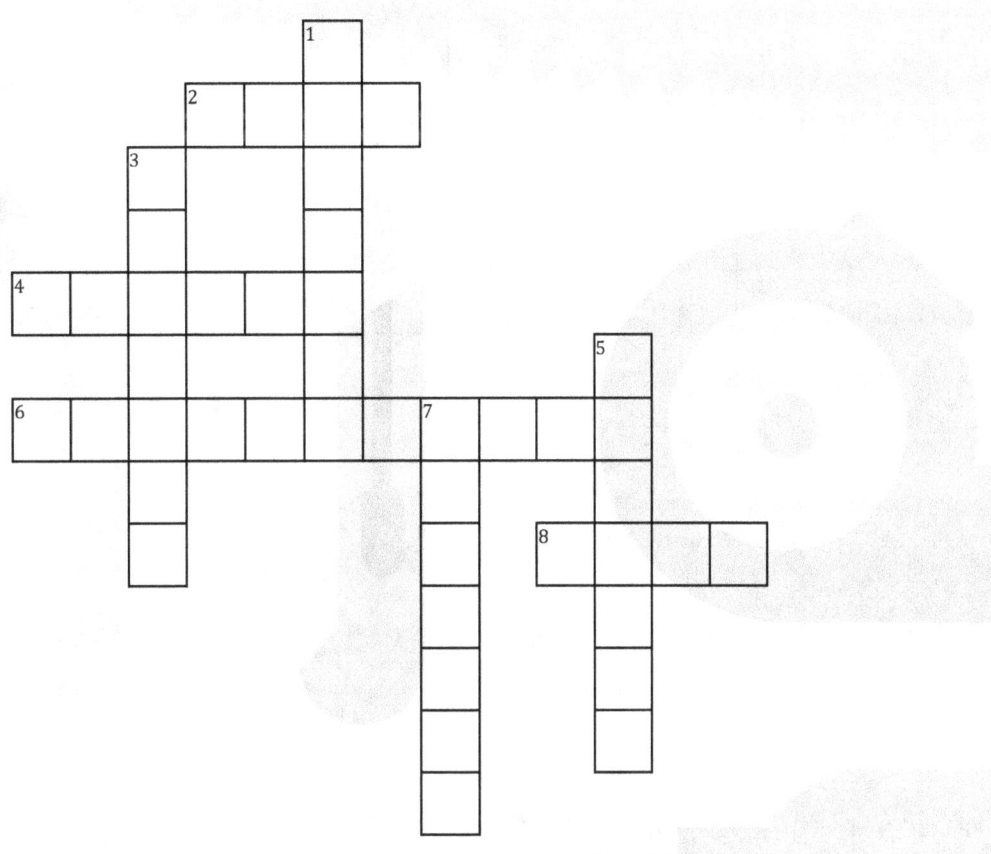

Across

2. A _____ is a group of people that work together towards a goal.

4. A _____ is a woman who has a child.

6. A _____ is a person who puts out fires and saves people's lives.

8. A _____ is someone who is admired for great courage, noble character, and performing good deeds, like a firefighter.

Down

1. _____ were Japanese warriors.

3. A _____ is a person who has had experience in an occupation. For example, ex-soldiers are often called _____s - especially those who have served in a war.

5. _____ are people who like and respect each other.

7. A _____ is a married man.

Body Parts

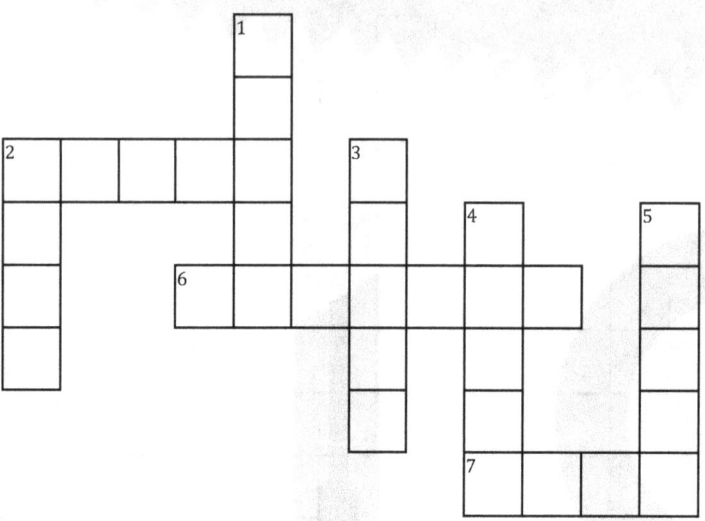

Across

2. It is the upper leg (thigh) bone. It is the longest bone in the human body.

6. These are dense patches of hair above the eyes.

7. It is the outer covering of our body.

Down

1. It is a special, high-energy picture of your bones or teeth.

2. We have five toes on each of these.

3. It is the joint in the middle of your arm.

4. These are hard, structural parts of the body of many animals. We have of these in our skeleton.

5. We think with this. It is protected by the skull.

Kitchen

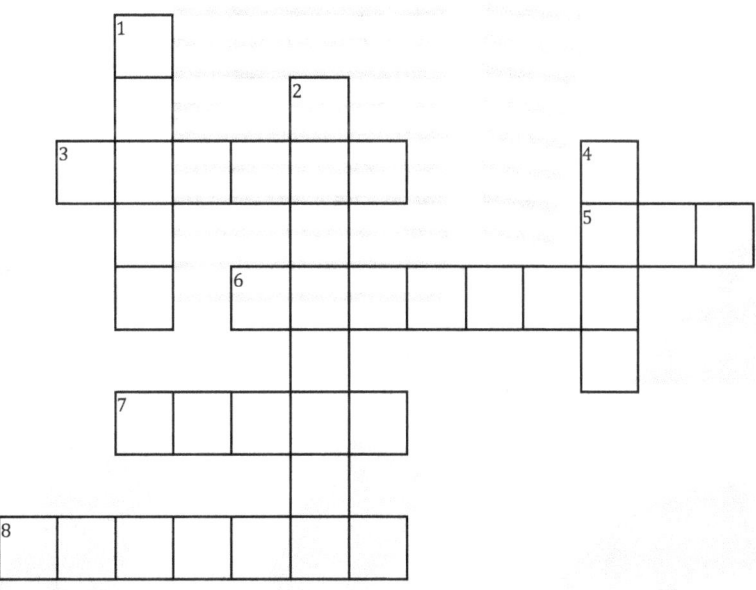

Across

3. _____ is a type of salty, spicy meat product, usually made from beef and/or pork.

5. _____ is a greasy liquid.

6. A _____ is a container for pouring liquids.

7. _____s are fruits that have a rind.

8. The _____ (or food chain) is all of the interactions between predators and prey in which plants and animals obtain food.

Down

1. _____es are sweet, juicy fruit with fuzzy skin.

2. An _____ is an animal that eats plants and meat. People are _____s

4. _____s are used for eating solid food.

Geography

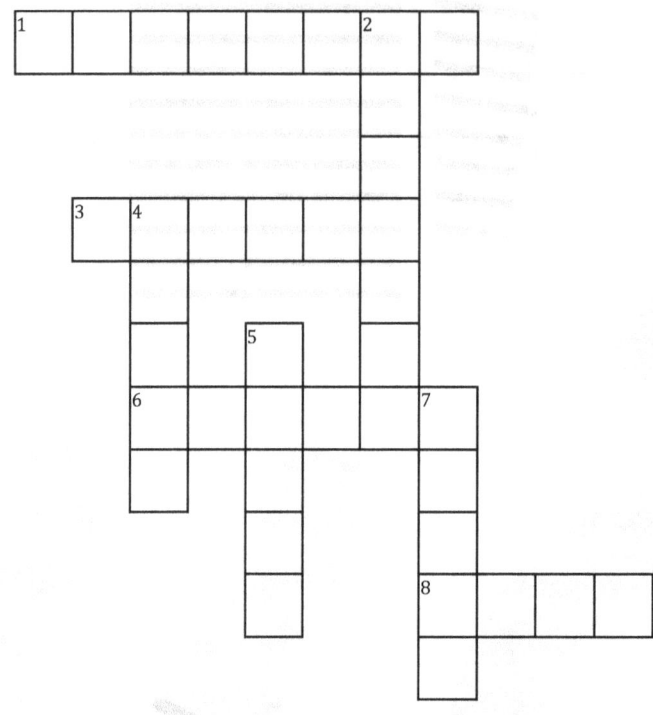

Across

1. Single large block of stone

3. Round pit at the summit of a volcano

6. Loose, rounded fragments of rock

8. Ocean waves that break on the shore or other land barriers.

Down

2. A flat surface covered with brick or concrete outside of a building.

4. System of connected mountains

5. A low, wet area, often thick with tall grasses; bog.

7. A fine-grained chalky soil, usually yellowish brown or gray, believed to consist of windblown dust.

Weather

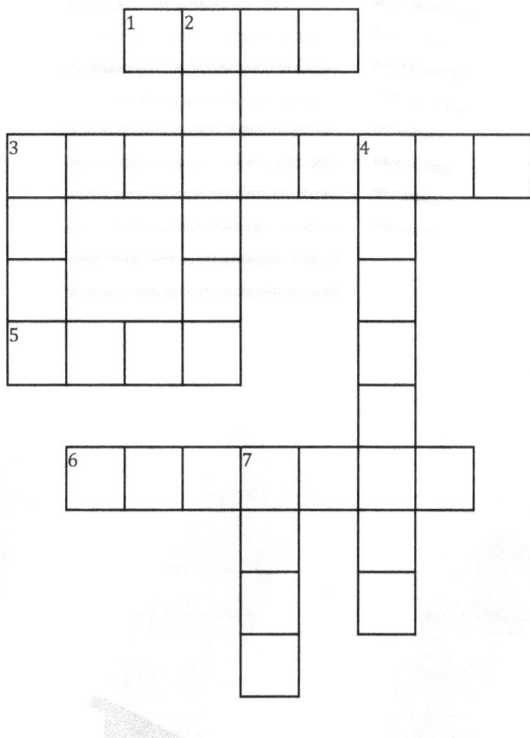

Across

1. Moderate wind storm

3. Intense, violent, rotating wind storm or tropical cyclone at sea

5. Molten rock that issues forth from the volcano

6. Seasonal wind storm that brings heavy rains to the Indian coast

Down

2. Bands or streamers of light that appear in the sky at night in areas around the magnetic poles, caused by solar particles striking atoms in the outer part of the earth's atmosphere.

3. Precipitation in the form of pellets of ice and hard snow

4. A report containing information and, often, a warning.

7. Fog augmented.

House

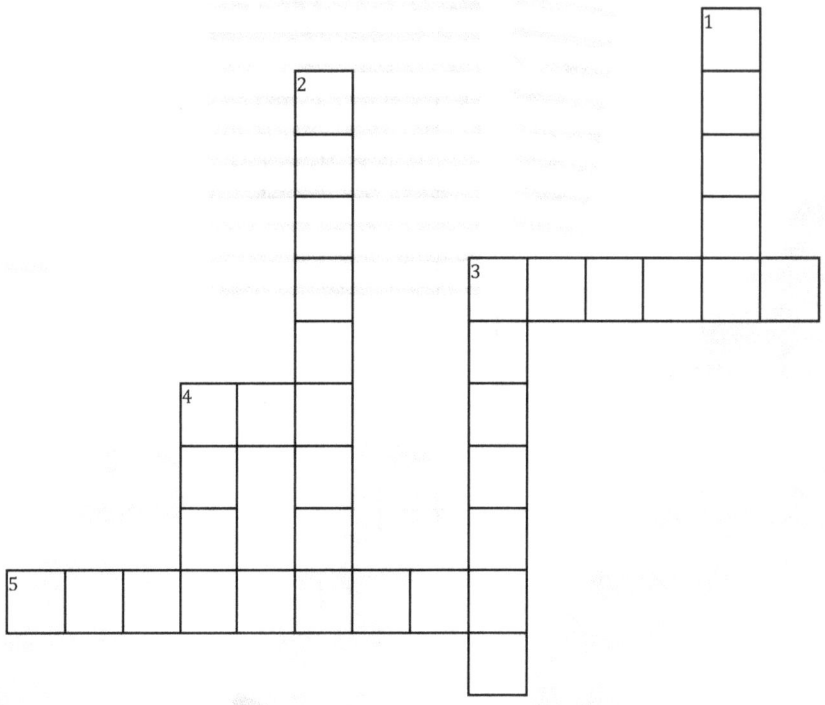

Across

3. A _____ is a floor covering made of woven yarn or thick fabric.

4. A _____ is a small, simple shelter.

5. You can make a fire in a _____ to keep you warm.

Down

1. People put pictures and photos in _____s to protect them and make them look nice.

2. A _____ is a small piece of furniture.

3. A _____ is a structure in which you can build a fire.

4. _____ is where you live.

Season

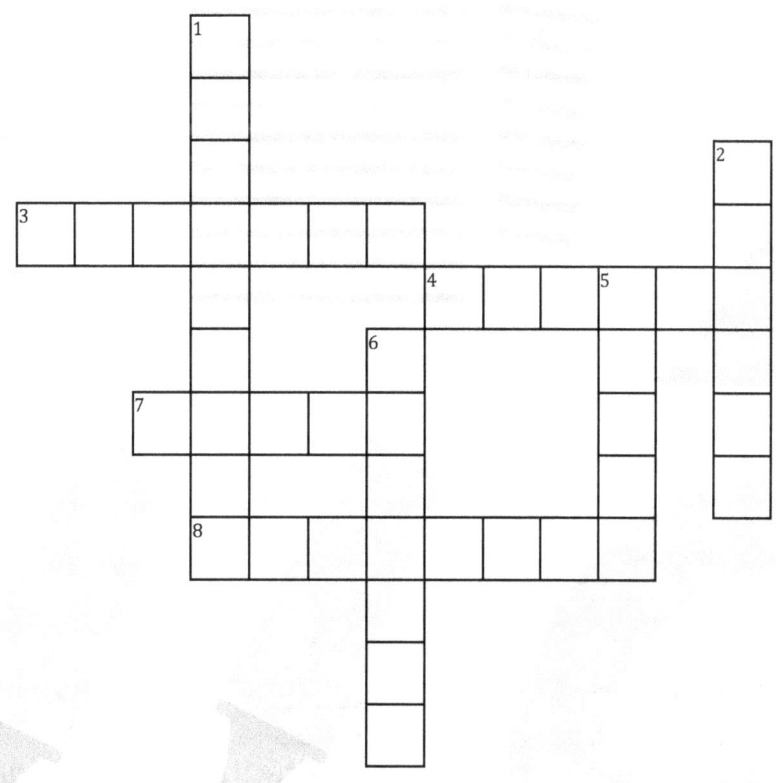

Across

3. A _____ is a large, slowly-moving river of ice.

4. You can tie a bow in a _____ to decorate something.

7. Spring starts during this month

8. _____ keep your ears warm.

Down

1. There are many kinds of me, including Reese's and Hershey's.

2. Open the ____ and let fresh air into the house

5. _____ are a type of shoe. _____ covers part of the lower leg.

6. A _____ is a structure in which you can build a fire.

Animals

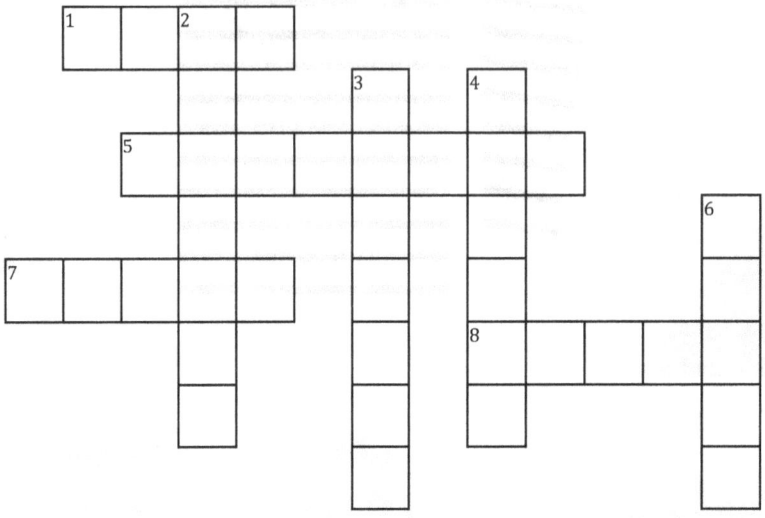

Across

1. A large wild cat with tan or gray fur and no spots. _____s live in many parts of North and South America. _____s are carnivorous mammals. They are also called cougars, mountain lions, or panthers.

5. A very small animal with a pointed nose and a very short tail. _____ have brown and yellow fur with spines that stick out and protect them when they roll into a ball. They make tunnels in rows of bushes called hedges.

7. A long, narrow animal that has smooth skin and no legs. _____s hunt and eat other animals. Some _____s are poisonous.

8. _____s are mammals that live in and around water. Unlike most other animals, _____s are playful even as adults. They like to slide down riverbanks and in snow.

Down

2. _____s are small mammals that are related to mongooses. They are known for the way they stand upright to watch for enemies. They are also known as sericites.

3. A large water bird that lives in warm areas. It has a pouch in the lower half of its long bill for catching and holding fish.

4. One of two kinds of vultures that are the largest flying birds of the western hemisphere. They have a bald head and neck, dark feathers, and can measure twelve feet across when they spread their wings.

6. The animals called _____s look like mice. But unlike mice, _____s are not rodents. Instead _____s belong to a group of insect-eating mammals called insectivores.

School

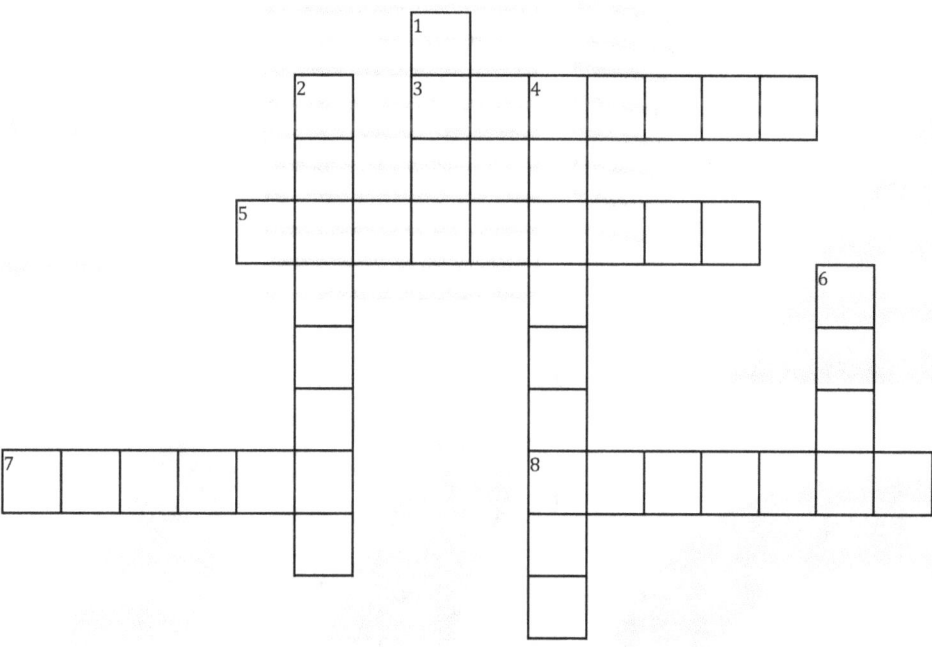

Across

3. The language of this country or a manner of speaking that language. _____ is also standard in various other countries such as the United States.

5. A collection of unbound papers or other printed material, often constituting a sample of one's professional work, intended to be shown to others and transported from place to place in a specially designed case.

7. What you say or write after someone asks you a question; a reply.

8. A person whose job or trade is printing.

Down

1. An examination or experiment to find out what something is, what it is made up of, or how good it is.

2. A strip of leather, ribbon, or paper placed between pages to mark a place in a book.

4. The science of the earth's surface and all life on it. When studying _____, one learns about the different countries and people of the earth, its climate, its natural resources, and its oceans, rivers, and mountains.

6. A thick, sticky liquid used to join things together.

Vacation

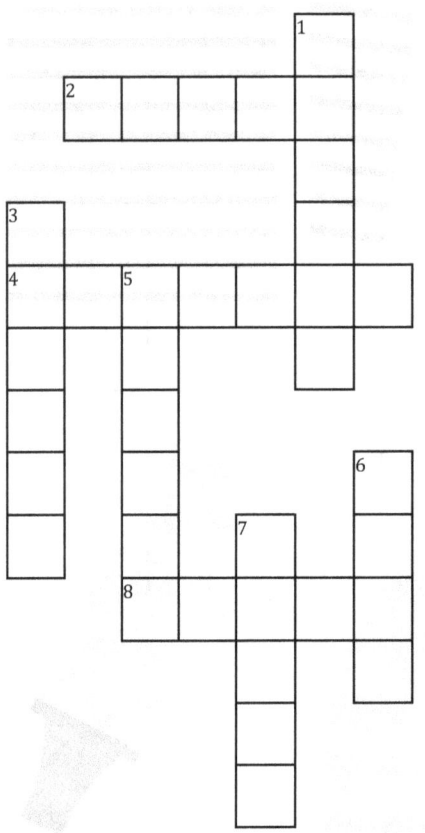

Across

2. A short form of the word "airplane."

4. A large area of level land where airplanes can land and take off.

8. A path or course through a forest or other rural place.

Down

1. To leave; go away.

3. An expedition for watching or hunting large animals.

5. A place where people go to relax and have fun while on vacation.

6. To lead or go with on foot.

7. A small house, usually built in a simple or rough way.

People

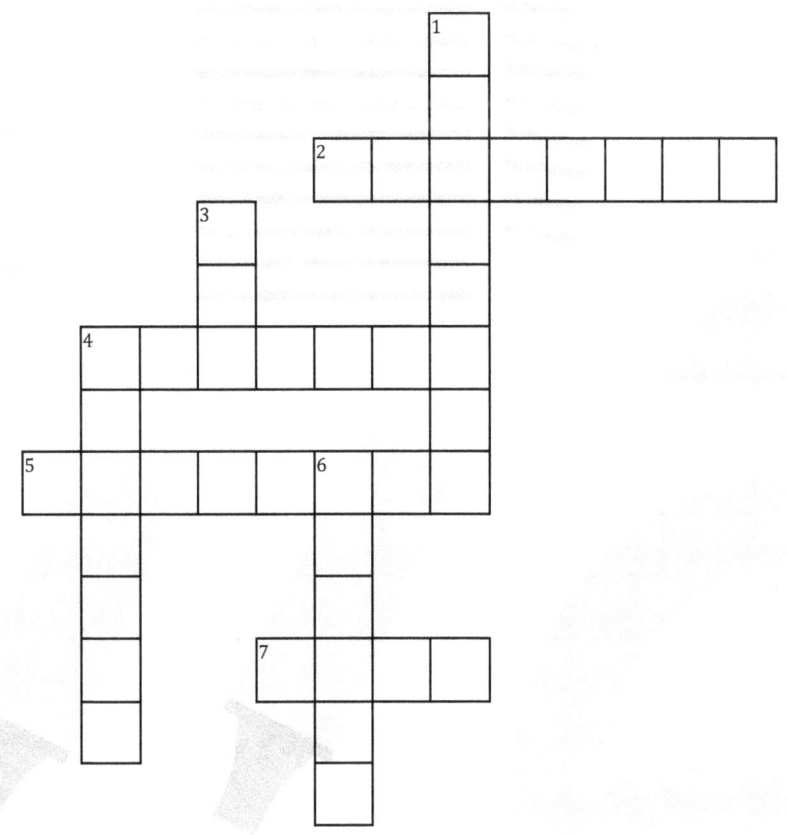

Across

2. A _____ is the daughter of a king or queen.

4. _____s are young children.

5. A _____ performs magic tricks.

7. A _____ is a woman.

Down

1. _____ are young people.

3. A _____ is a young person.

4. A _____ is someone who helps you learn.

6. An _____ is a baby.

Body Parts

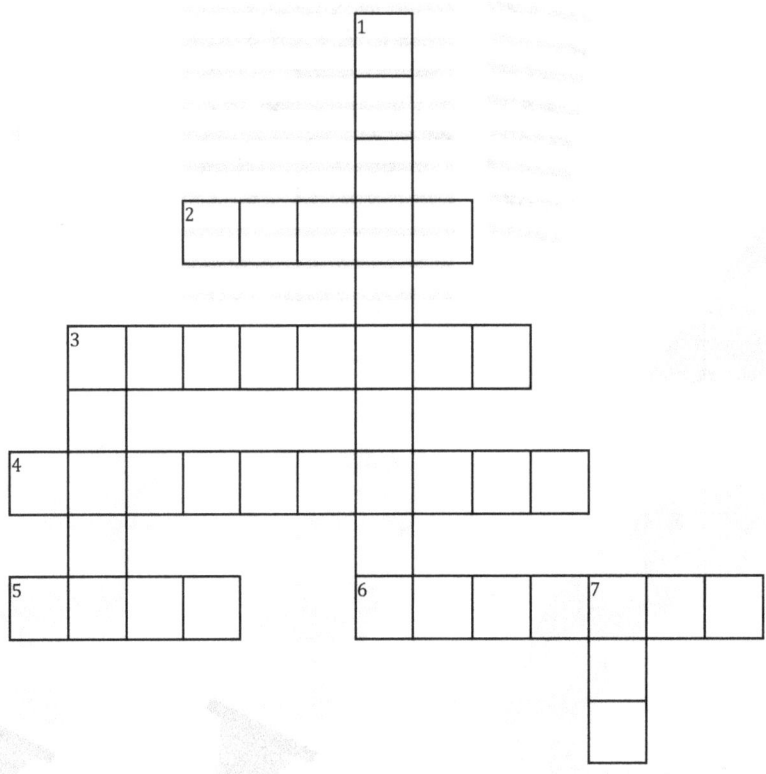

Across

2. It is an animal that walks on two legs.

3. It is the set of bones in a body.

4. It grows at the ends of your fingers.

5. It is the back part of the foot.

6. It is a pouch-like organ that is part of the digestive system. It helps digest food by churning it in an acid bath.

Down

1. These are parts of the digestive system. These help digest food, absorb it into the body, and excrete waste.

3. The _____ (also called the backbone) is a series of connected bones in the back that surround and protect the spinal cord.

7. You can carry things in your _____.

Kitchen

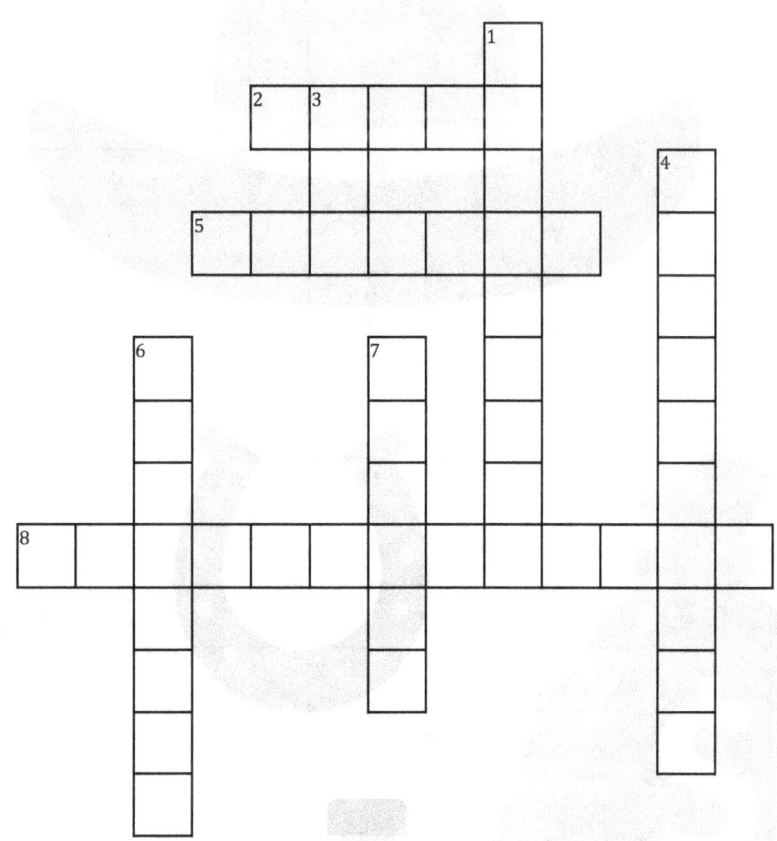

Across

2. You can cook food on a _____.

5. A _____ is a machine that heats up slices of bread, making toast.

8. _____s heat up food quickly.

Down

1. _____s are edible plants, like spinach, celery, and kale; they very good for you.

3. _____ is a drink that is brewed from _____ leaves.

4. The _____ is a sweet, red fruit.

6. _____ is a type of squash.

7. _____ grows in warm weather.

Geography

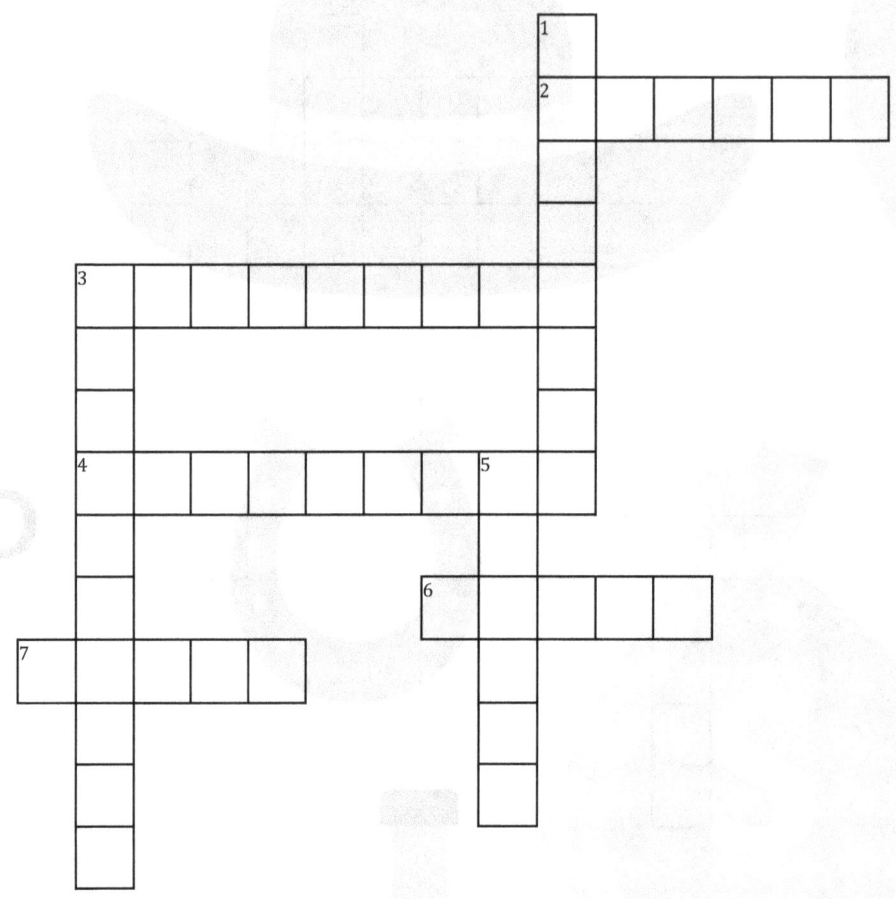

Across

2. A deep, narrow valley. _____s are usually created by flowing water.

3. A piece of land surrounded on nearly all sides by water. It is connected to a larger body of land by a usually narrow strip of land.

4. A stony or metallic mass of matter that has fallen to the earth's surface from outer surface

6. A narrow part like a shelf that comes out of a wall.

7. Coral island

Down

1. Deep crack in glacial ice

3. A high cliff that sticks out into a large body of water or that rises above an area of lower land.

5. Long and deep trough in ocean floor bordering few continents

Weather

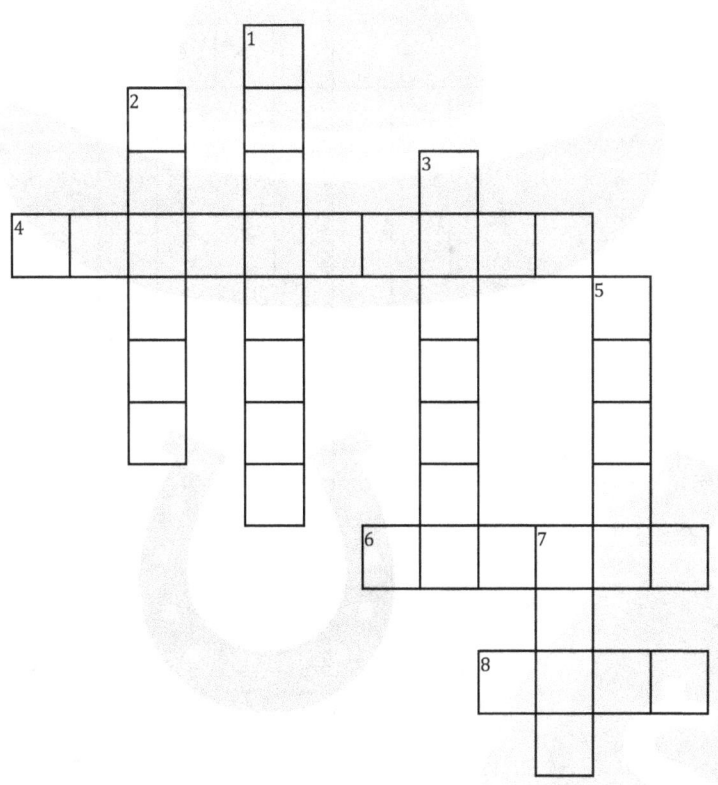

Across

4. Sudden, intense rainfall
6. Gentle breeze from the west
8. Continuous flow of water resulting in flood

Down

1. The ocean belt near the equator, characterized by calms and light, variable winds, or the characteristic weather of this region.

2. A period of rain that lasts a short time.

3. Very light rain

5. Warm and damp so as to make breathing difficult.

7. A circle of light shining around the head of a god, an angel, or a saint in a picture.

Business

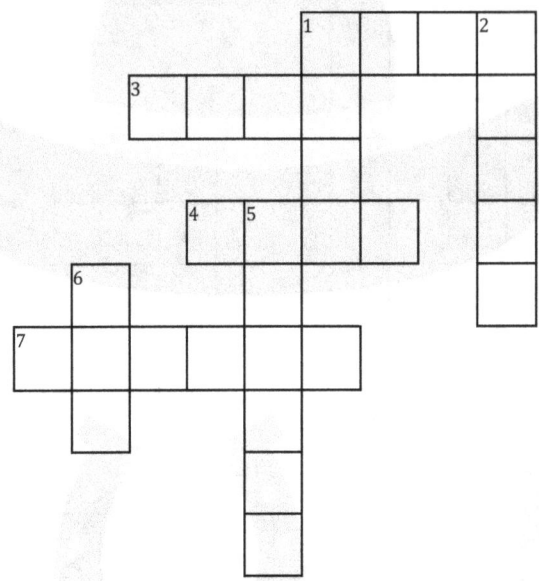

Across

1. Something that shows a fact, event, or some other thing.

3. To let go or dismiss from a job.

4. An exchange of goods for money; the act of selling.

7. Someone who does a job or has a job.

Down

1. To give something to someone in exchange for money.

2. A job or activity that seems just right for a particular person.

5. A list of things to be done or talked about.

6. Work a person does every day or every week and gets paid for.

Season

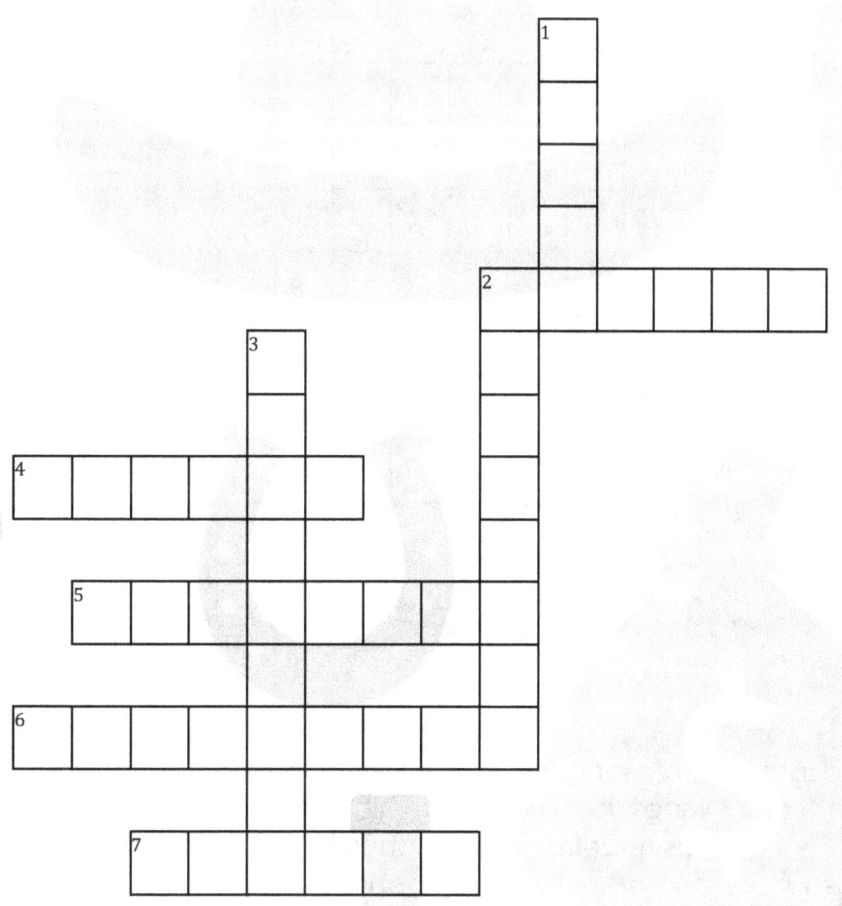

Across

2. I am beautiful, and bees love me!

4. Rain gathers in one spot on the ground and makes a _____

5. Hold this to stay dry when it rains

6. A caterpillar turns into a _____

7. The season that comes before summer.

Down

1. _____ showers bring may flowers.

2. _____ is the second month of the year.

3. _____s are large meat-eaters live in the far north. They have clear-colored hair and black skin.

Animals

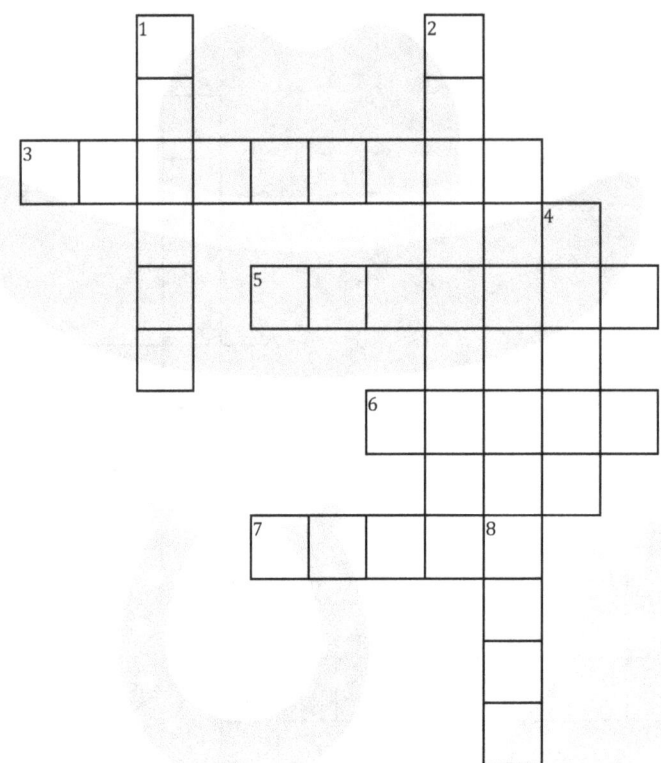

Across

3. A brightly colored insect with a long, narrow body. It has four long, clear wings that are held out from the body. _____ lives near fresh water and eats mosquitoes and other insects.

5. A large, wild cat of Africa and Southern Asia that has solid black spots on its fur. _____s have long legs and are the fastest animal on land. Sometimes they are trained for hunting game.

6. A large, strong mammal in the cat family that has light fur with black stripes.

7. A large animal with long legs and a long neck. _____s are domesticated mammals; people use _____s for riding and for carrying loads across deserts. _____s from the deserts of Central Asia have two humps. _____s from Northern Africa and the middle east have one hump.

Down

1. A large rodent, up to four feet long, with thick brown fur and a wide flat tail. _____ use their long front teeth to cut down trees for food and to build dams and lodges. They use the dams to keep water around their lodges. _____ lives in North America, Europe, and Asia.

2. The _____ is a mammal of the weasel family. Like its relative the skunk, the _____ can give off an unpleasant smell. It is sometimes called a skunk bear.

4. A large, shiny, black bird that looks like a crow. It makes a sound like a loud, sharp croak.

8. A mammal in the cat family with soft, spotted fur, pointed ears, and a short tail. Several kinds of _____ live in Europe, North America, and Asia. They are carnivores and are related to other wild cats. _____ are about twice the size of house cats.

School

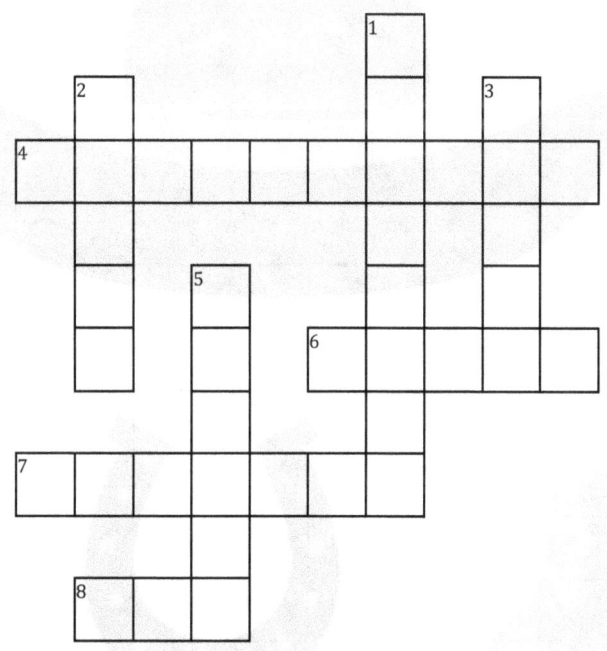

Across

4. Usually colored white, used as a writing surface in places such as classrooms and meeting rooms. _____ are used in a way similar to blackboards, but they have a smooth, shiny surface that is designed to be written on with special markers and easily erased.

6. A stand for holding an artist's canvas, blackboard, or sign.

7. Everything that has happened in the past to people or things, or a telling of these events.

8. A picture of an area of the earth or sky drawn or printed on a flat surface.

Down

1. A list of unusual or difficult words and their meanings connected with a particular subject or particular piece of writing. A _____ is often placed at the end of a book.

2. A substance made from natural _____ that is formed into round sticks that can be used to write or draw with, especially on a blackboard or on pavement.

3. A number or letter given on schoolwork to show quality or correctness.

5. Shortened form of "_____ computer."

Vacation

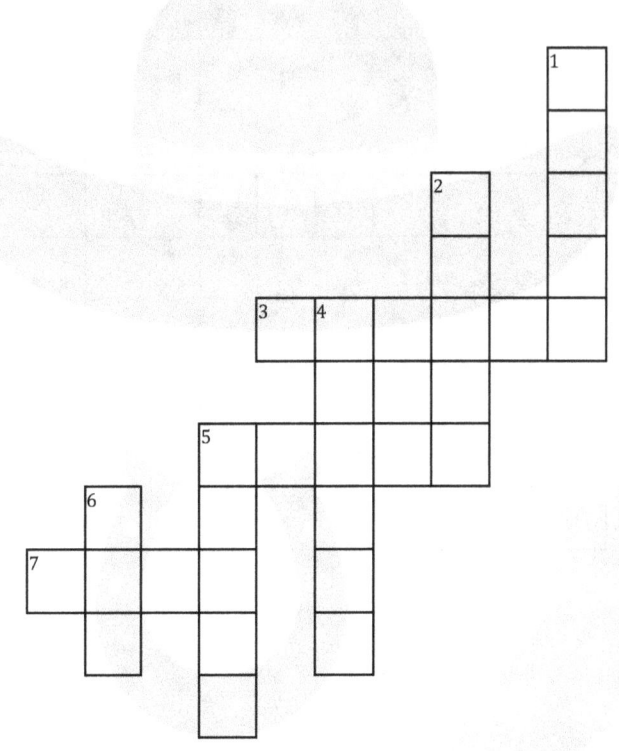

Across

3. To board a ship when beginning a trip.

5. To go or come to see.

7. The solid part of the earth's surface.

Down

1. The main stem of a tree.

2. A sheet that gives information in the form of a graph or table.

4. A building where collections of objects that are important to history, art, or science are kept and shown to the public.

5. A recording of pictures and sounds to be played on a television or computer.

6. A car that carries people who need a ride and who pay money for it.

People

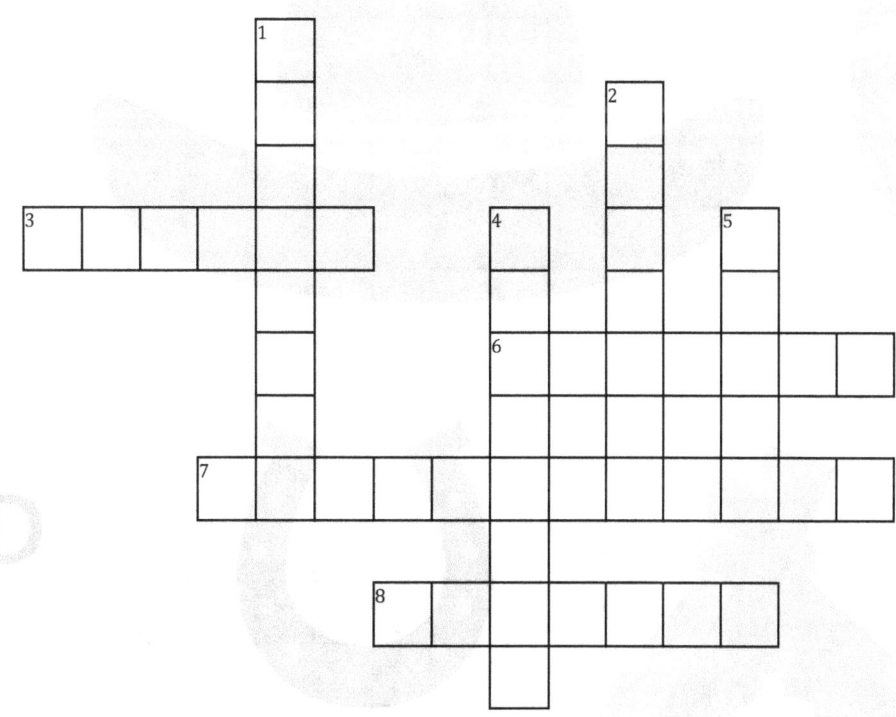

Across

3. _____s are girls or women who have the same parents.

6. Someone who is good at a sport is an _____.

7. _____ are grandmothers and grandfathers.

8. _____s are boys or men who have the same parents.

Down

1. An _____ designs and creates new, useful things.

2. A _____ is someone who throws a ball or other item.

4. A _____ is the winner of a game or other competition.

5. A _____ is a hereditary ruler of a country.

Kitchen

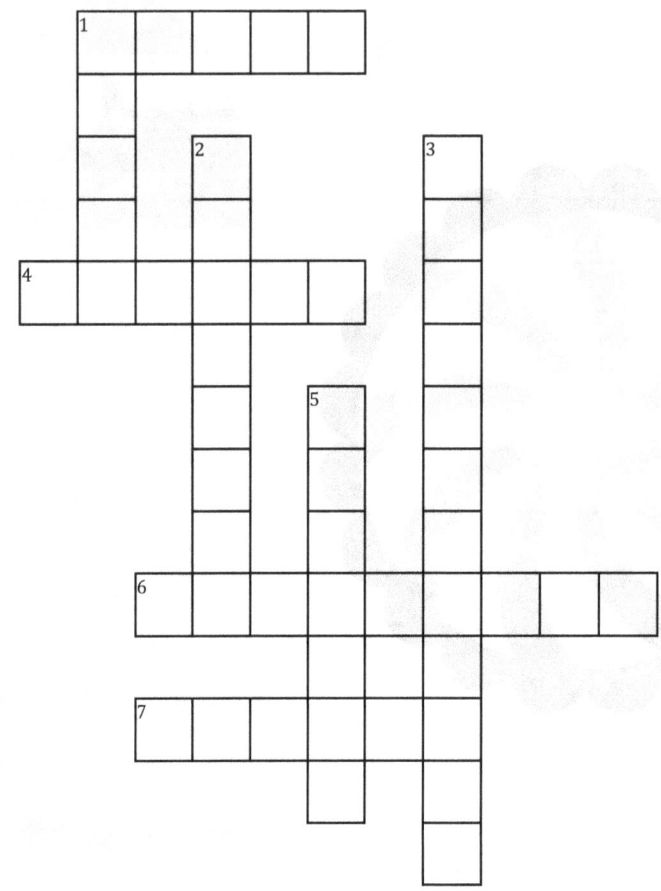

Across

1. A _____ is a rock.

4. Peas grow in _____s.

6. A _____ is a sweet, juicy fruit with smooth skin; it is related to the peach.

7. An _____ is a dish made from eggs.

Down

1. When something is _____d, thin pieces are cut from it.

2. A _____ is a sweet, frozen treat on a stick.

3. A _____ is a machine that keeps food cold.

5. A _____ is a tool that has a wide, flat end.

Geography

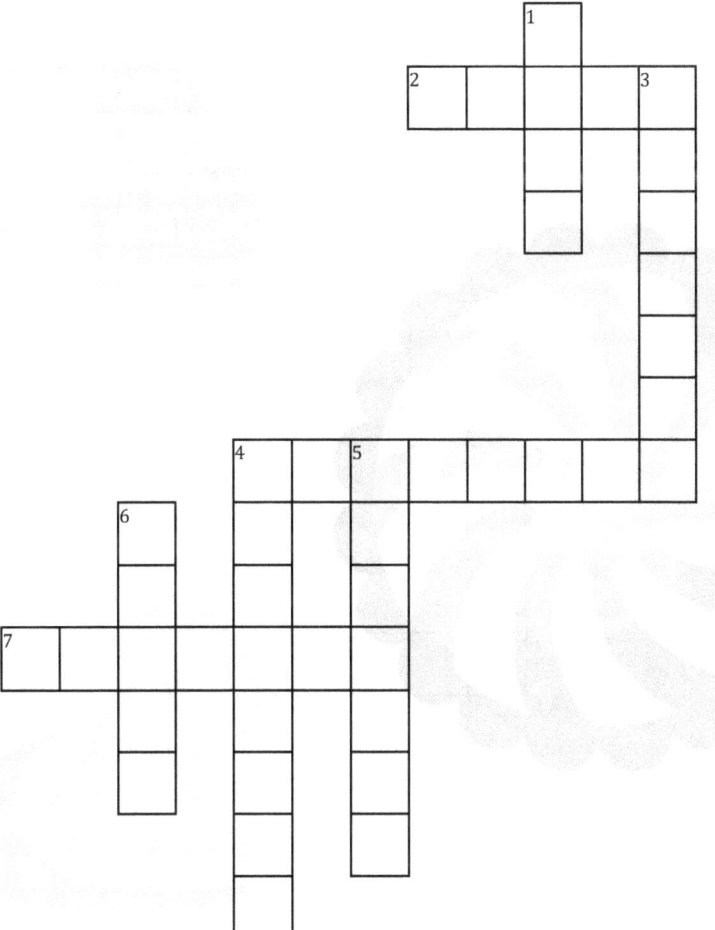

Across

2. A low area of land that is covered with water.

4. The distance between the equator and a point north or south on the earth's surface. This distance is measured in degrees.

7. A large mass of rock

Down

1. Hollow area in earth with opening at the surface

3. A large area of fertile land covered with grass.

4. Any of the earth's topographic features, such as a hill or valley, that have been formed by natural forces of movement, erosion, or the like.

5. Land or ground, or the natural characteristics of its surface.

6. A raised amount of something; pile.

Weather

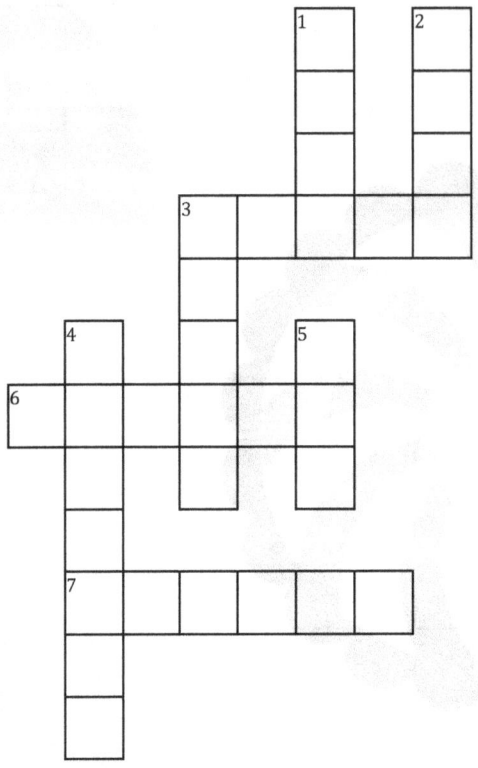

Across

3. Freezing rain.

6. A light fall of snow that ends quickly.

7. Rain cloud of uniform gray that covers the entire sky

Down

1. The water that rises from the surface of a body of water.

2. Sudden, sharp burst of wind

3. A violent event in weather. In a _____, there may be a lot of rain, snow, or wind.

4. A book published every year that predicts the weather for each day and gives facts about the tides, the time the sun will rise and set, and other useful information.

5. A calm region at the center of storm or cyclone or hurricane

Business

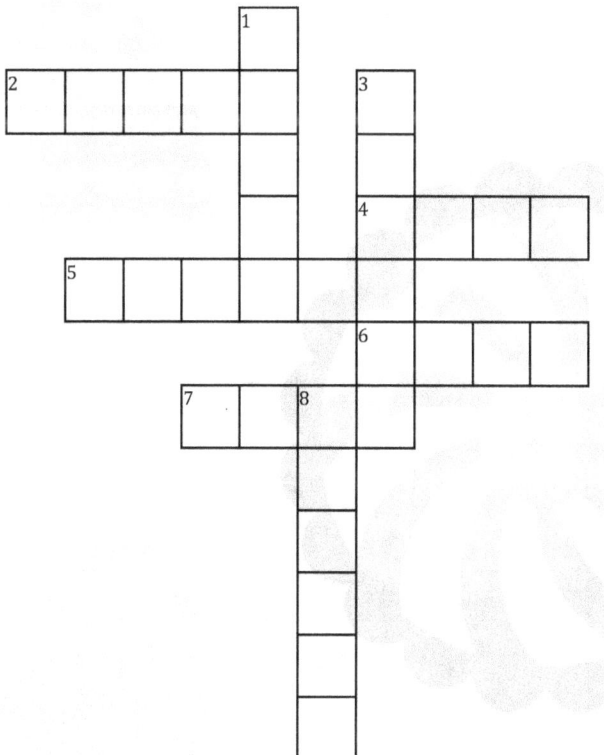

Across

2. To shut.

4. A privilege or benefit, as of a high rank or position; perquisite.

5. A computer that is portable and suitable for use while traveling.

6. A decrease in size or amount.

7. Something that a person should do because it is right or fair.

Down

1. An amount of money taken out of or owed on an account.

3. To provide what is wanted or needed.

8. A government tax on goods that come into a country; duty.

Season

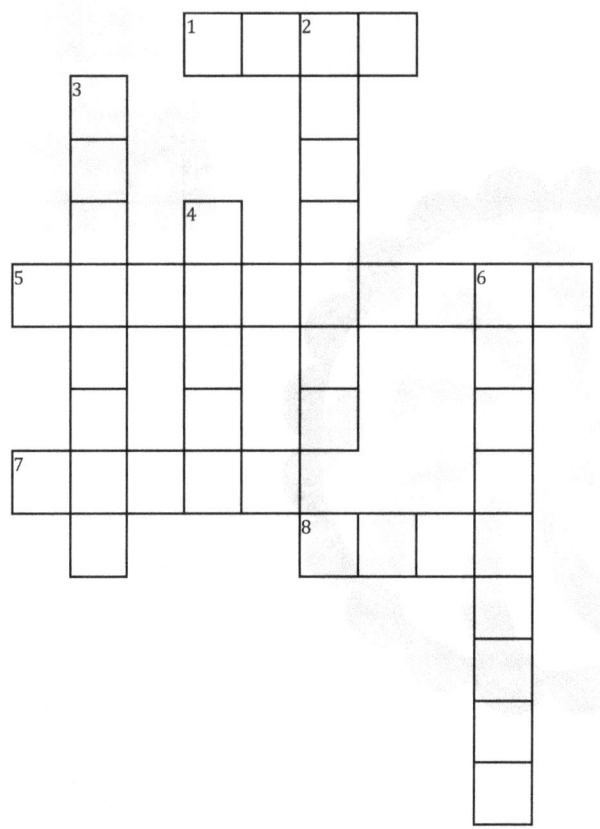

Across

1. Children go to the _____ and play

5. I am a type of candy that is colorful and delicious.

7. Some kinds of me are peeps and taffy.

8. Ice and snow _____

Down

2. Colorful arc in the sky after the rain

3. A _____ lets you know what day it is.

4. _____s are white or gray object that floats in the air and contains tiny water drops or ice particles.

6. A _____ is a long, loose garment worn to bed.

Animals

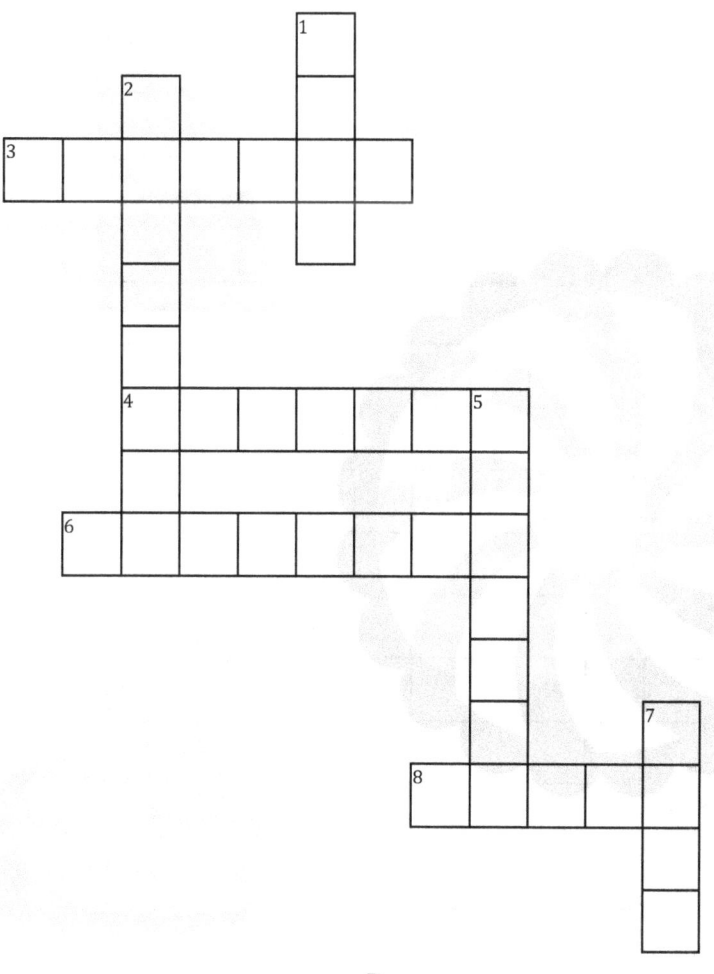

Across

3. A small bird with brown or gray feathers. _____s are very common in north America.

4. A small, round beetle that is red or orange with black spots. _____s eat aphids and other insects that are harmful to plants.

6. _____s are curious-looking animals. Their long heads and snouts look like tubes, and they have no teeth at all.

8. A large black-and-white mammal that is related to bears. They live in the mountains of western china and eat only bamboo plants. They are also called giant _____s.

Down

1. A large, strong mammal in the cat family that lives in Africa and Asia. Male _____s have long hair around the head and neck.

2. _____s are shy mammals that are not seen very often. They are mostly active at night.

5. A very large ape that lives in African forests. _____s are the largest of the primates. Male _____s living in zoos can weigh as much as six hundred pounds. All _____s living in the wild are in danger of extinction.

7. A large bird with a short beak and sharp claws. _____s catch and eat small animals.

School

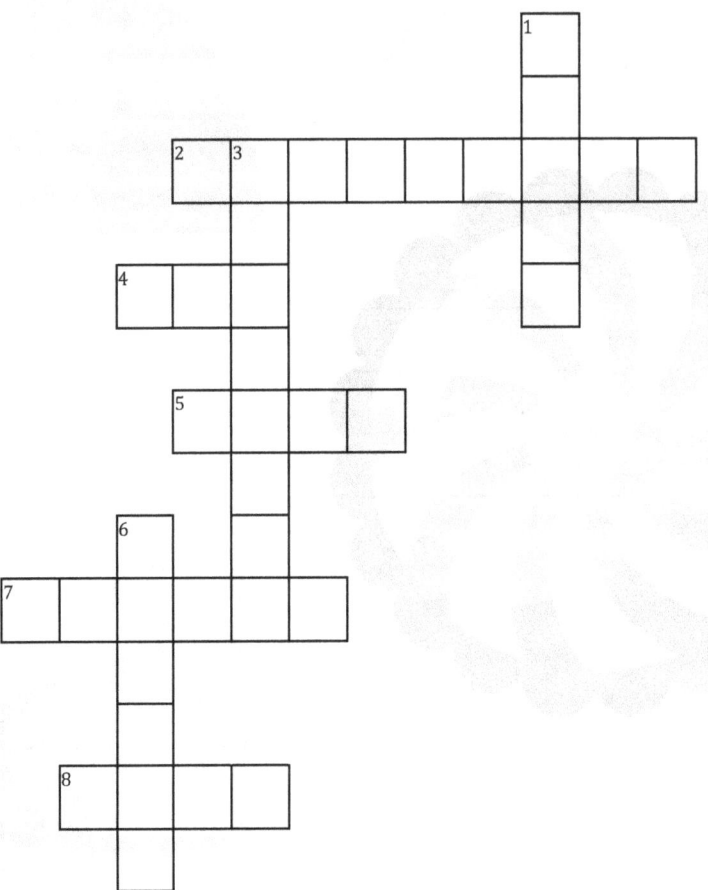

Across

2. A room in a school or college where classes are held.

4. A long, thin tool used for writing or drawing in ink.

5. A short or informal test.

7. A pen, usually with a felt tip, that makes thick lines of ink and is used for writing and drawing.

8. Sheets of paper bound together between two covers. These pages can be blank or can have writing, printing, or pictures on them.

Down

1. A round ball with a map of the earth on it, or anything shaped like a ball.

3. A way to communicate without using words.

6. A colored stick or pencil made of wax. A _____ is used for drawing and coloring.

People

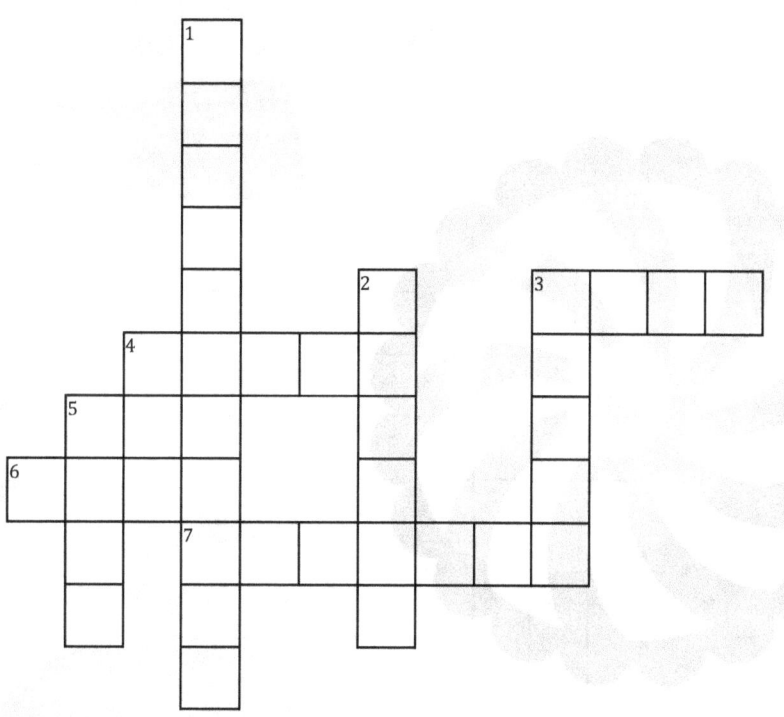

Across

3. A _____ is a very young person.

4. A _____ takes care of you when you are sick or hurt.

6. A _____ is a young woman.

7. An _____ is an unelected ruler of a country.

Down

1. _____ are four siblings (brothers and/or sisters) who are born at the same time from the same mother.

2. A _____ was an entertainer for royalty during the middle ages.

3. A _____ bakes food in the oven, like breads, cakes, and cookies.

5. A _____ is a married woman.

Kitchen

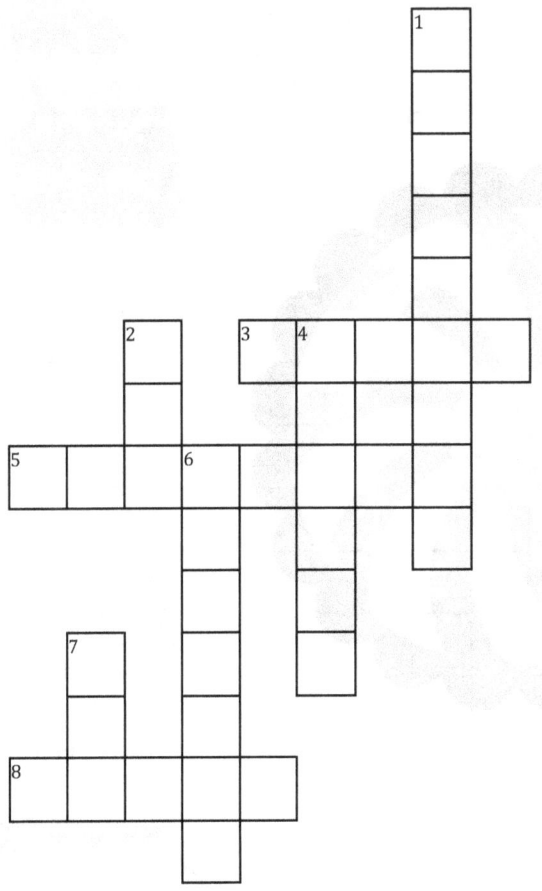

Across

3. A _____ is used for eating food like soup and cereal.

5. _____ is a drink made from water, lemon juice, and sugar.

8. A _____ is a hollow tube that is used to drink liquids.

Down

1. A _____ is a plant that turns to face the sun.

2. _____s are sweet vegetables that grow underground.

4. _____s grow underground; they are a type of legume.

6. _____ is a cereal.

7. People cook food in _____s.

Animals

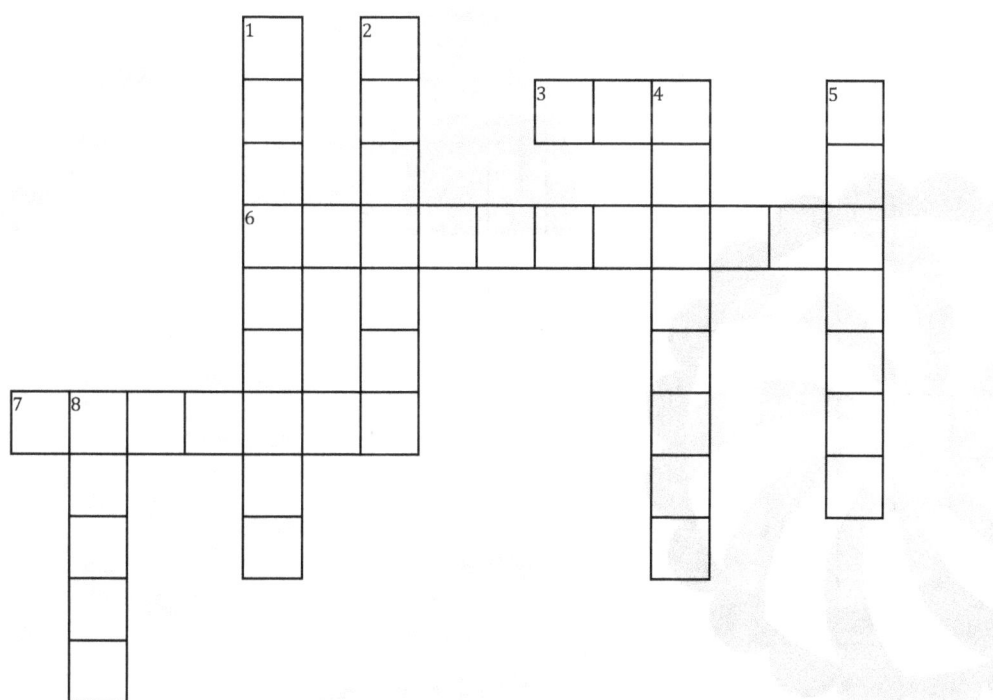

Across

3. A kind of mammal with four legs and a tail. People keep _____s as pets. Some _____s help people guard buildings or animals such as sheep.

6. The larva, or middle life stage, of a moth or butterfly. _____s are round and long like worms, but have six legs. They may be brightly colored.

7. An insect that eats wood. _____ have pale, soft bodies and look somewhat like ants. They live in large groups in warmer parts of the world. They can destroy trees, buildings, and other things made out of wood.

Down

1. A large reptile that is found in tropical swamps. It has a thick, tough skin, a long tail, and a long, pointed snout.

2. A large bird that usually has dark feathers and a bald head and neck. These birds are related to hawks and feed on dead animals.

4. A small fish that lives in fresh water. _____ Are usually yellow or orange and are often kept in ponds or aquariums.

5. A mammal with a very long neck, long legs, and hooves.

8. A large, strong bird that hunts small animals and fish.

Weather

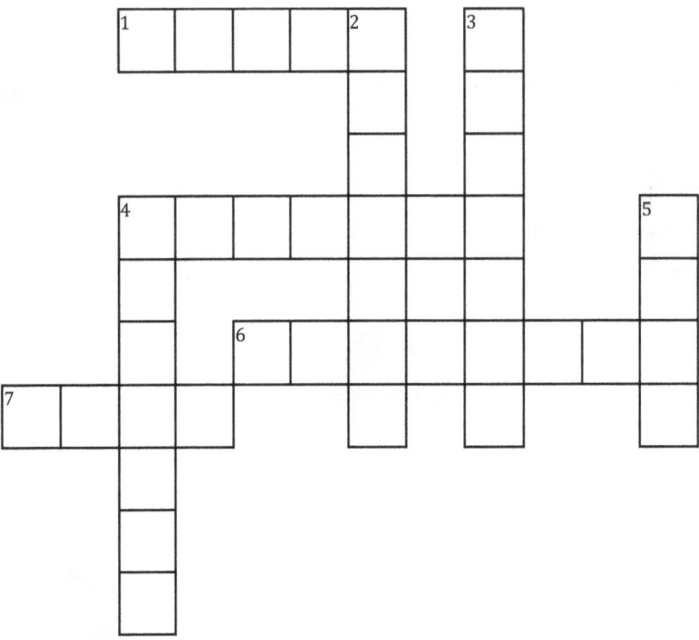

Across

1. Minute ice crystals that form on surfaces

4. The conditions outside. _____ concerns such things as temperature, rain, snow, sun, and other things.

6. An accumulation of fallen snow.

7. An area that is separate or different from other areas because of a particular environment, use, or some other special quality.

Down

2. A hurricane that occurs in the western pacific area and the china sea.

3. An upward current of air.

4. A message in words, sound, or action that warns of something bad.

5. Not moving; still.

Business

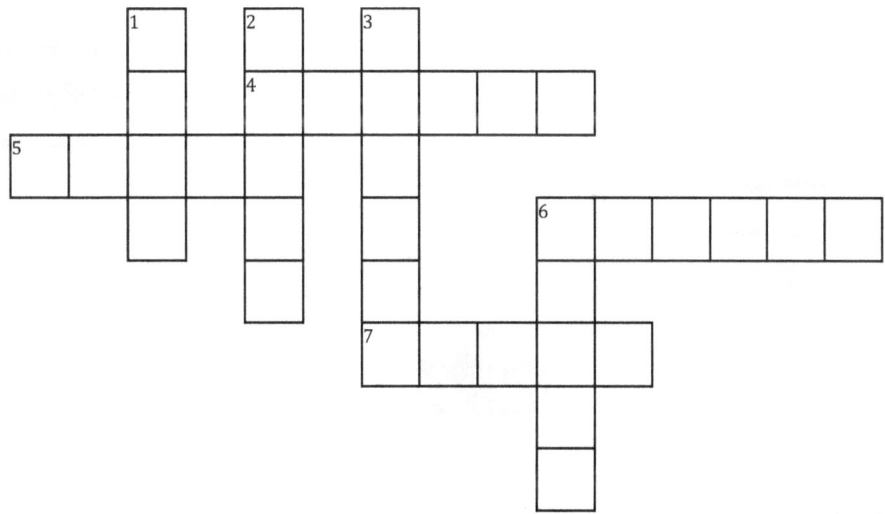

Across

4. A thing that you aim at and want to hit.

5. The goods carried by a ship, airplane, or other vehicle.

6. To take something and promise to return it.

7. A general course, direction, or tendency.

Down

1. A period of time during which something happens.

2. Things that you keep that are ready for use or for sale at any time; supply.

3. The right or ability to buy things now but not pay until later.

6. A payment added to a person's regular pay as a reward for hard work.

Season

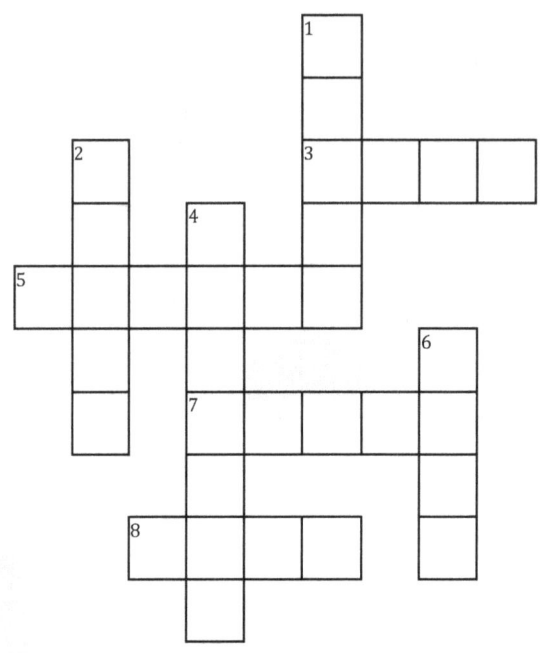

Across

3. The Easter bunny hides me!

5. A _____ is a silky covering made by a caterpillar. The _____ protects the developing moth.

7. An Inuit hut, shaped like a dome and made of blocks of ice or hard snow.

8. Balls of ice that fall from clouds are called _____ or _____ stones.

Down

1. Grass grows and turns the color _____

2. _____ is a white owl that lives in the north American tundra (a cold, snowy environment).

4. A _____ is a time to celebrate. Some _____ s are new year's, Mother's Day, veteran's day, Independence Day, and Thanksgiving Day.

6. We shiver when it is _____.

Animals

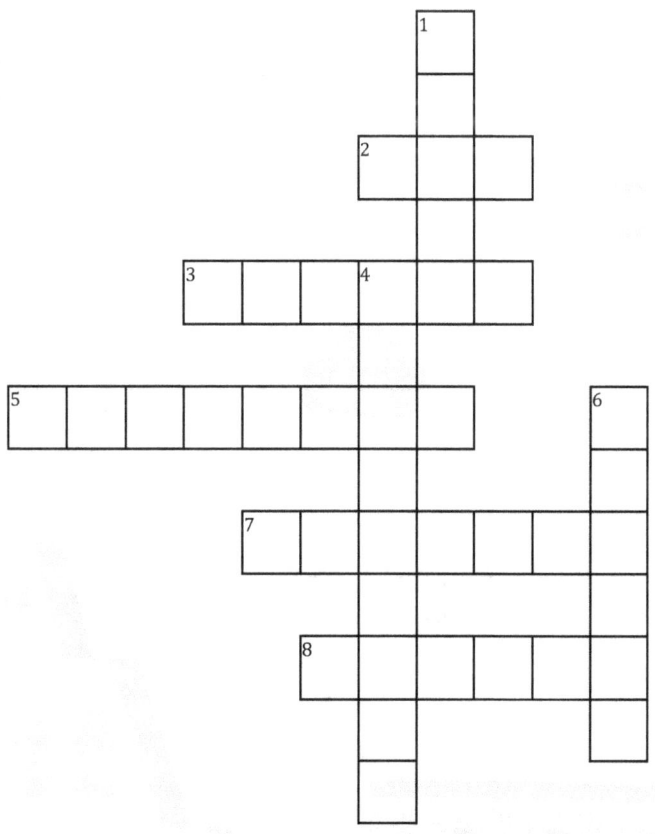

Across

2. _____s are the only mammals that can truly fly. Sometimes people mistake _____s for birds. But _____s are more closely related to other mammals—including humans.

3. The _____ is a north American wild cat. Its name comes from its tail, which looks "bobbed," or cut short. The _____ is sometimes called a bay lynx.

5. A young duck.

7. A common bird that people raise on farms for its meat and eggs.

8. An insect with a pair of hard front wings that covers a pair of thin wings. There are many different kinds of _____s. Japanese _____s, ladybugs, and fireflies are _____s.

Down

1. An animal with long legs and a long neck. _____s are mammals that live in the mountains of south America. They are closely related to camels but are smaller. _____s are raised for their meat, milk, and wool.

4. A small animal with a narrow body like a worm. A _____'s body is divided into many segments, each having a pair of legs. The front legs have poison claws. _____s are a kind of arthropod and are active at night.

6. An adult male goose.

83

School

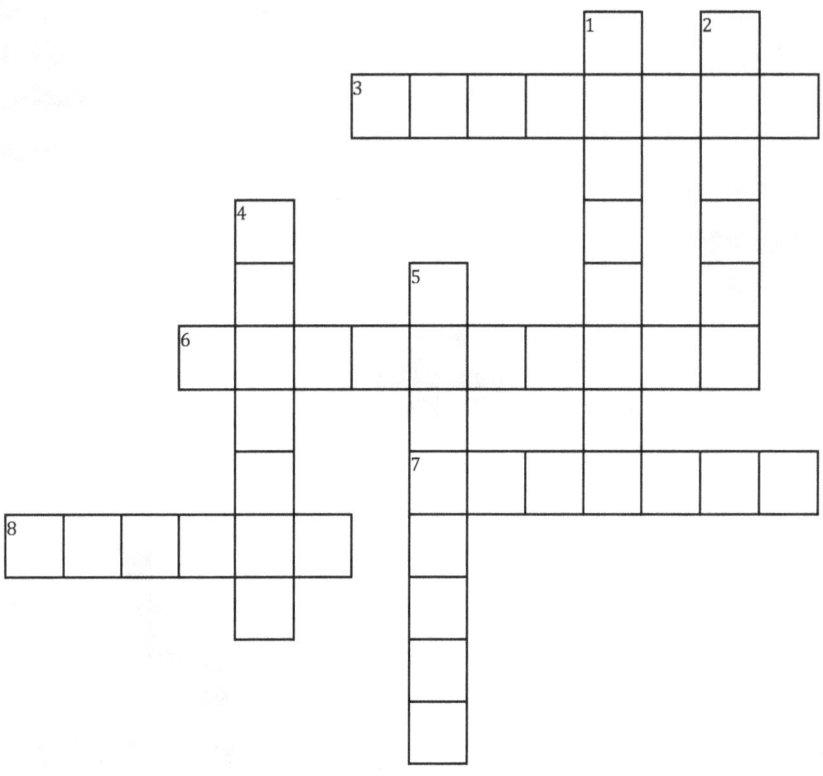

Across

3. A row or rows of keys. Pianos, typewriters, and computers have _____s.

6. A machine used in computing numbers.

7. To make thinner or finer, as a cutting edge or point.

8. A piece of paper or cardboard folded at the center. A _____ can hold papers or letters.

Down

1. An electronic device that is used to store and sort information and work with data at a high speed.

2. An object used to erase or rub out writing or marks.

4. A tool in a home or office that uses staples to attach papers together.

5. To ask for answers about something.

People

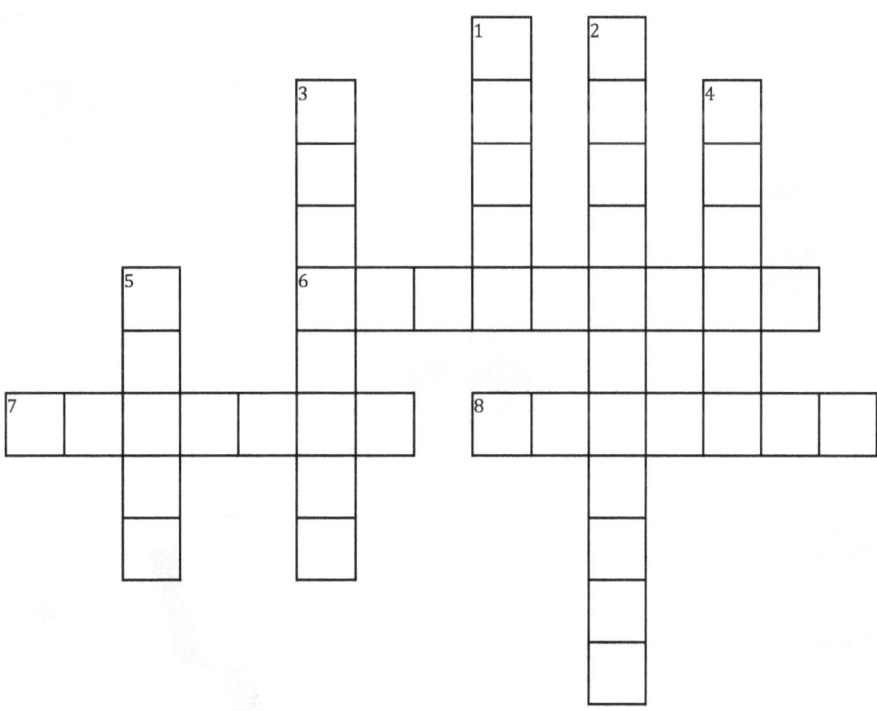

Across

6. A _____ is the elected leader of a country or organization.

7. A _____ is a person who fights for a country.

8. A _____ is a person who is the first to do something, like settle in a new area or do research.

Down

1. _____ are two siblings (brothers and/or sisters) who are born at the same time.

2. The mother of your father or mother is your _____.

3. _____ are three siblings (brothers and/or sisters) who are born at the same time.

4. A _____ is the son of a king or queen.

5. A _____ is person who is mean to others.

Geography

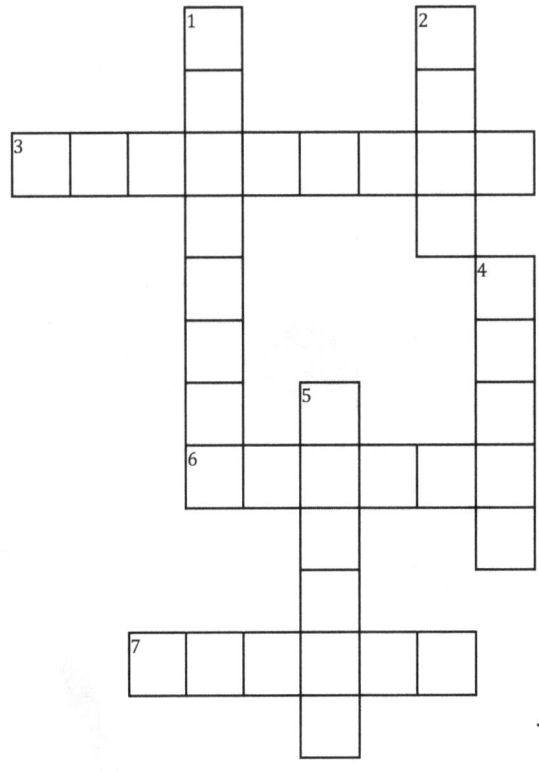

Across

3. A large landmass on the surface of earth

6. Water mixture of insoluble mud and lime

7. A flow of water from the earth.

Down

1. Loose fragments of rock

2. Peak of volcano

4. The flat floor of a usually dry desert lake.

5. The highest part.

Weather

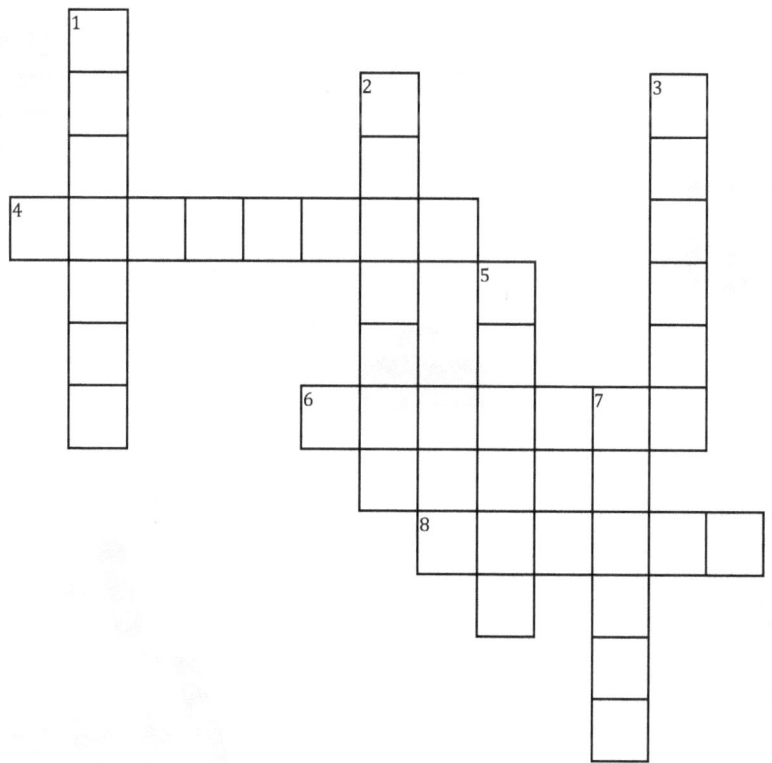

Across

4. Violent snow storm

6. The moment each day at which the sun first can be seen above the eastern horizon.

8. The season of the year between summer and winter; fall.

Down

1. Violent, rotating wind storm

2. A low-lying extended gray cloud formation with a relatively flat bottom.

3. Gentle wind

5. A type of cloud that usually appears in the form of strings or threads.

7. A sudden, powerful wind that moves in suddenly. It usually brings rain, snow, or sleet.

Kitchen

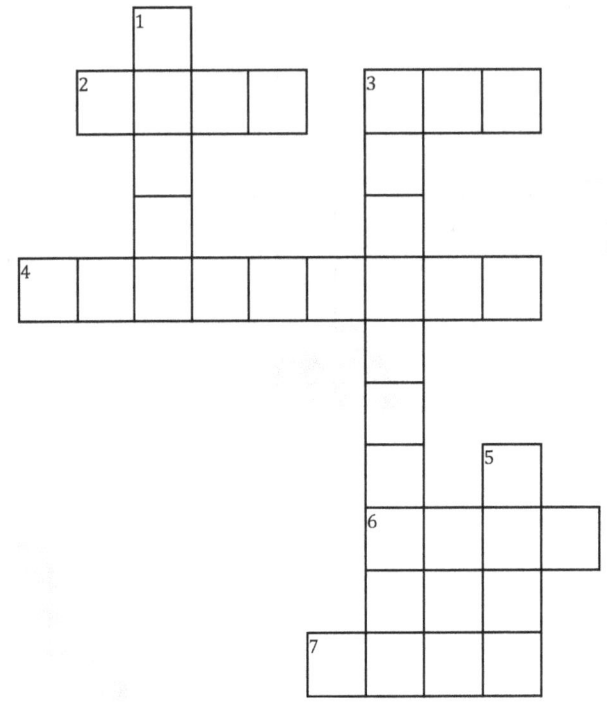

Across

2. The _____ of an egg is yellow and contains stored food for a bird or reptile before it hatches.

3. Peas grow in pea _____s.

4. You can cook food in a _____.

6. _____ are small, round vegetables.

7. _____ is a type of food that comes from animals. Some types of _____ are beef and ham.

Down

1. _____ is a sweet substance made by bees.

3. _____ is a dessert made from pumpkins.

5. _____ is an important crystalline mineral that we use to season our food.

Animals

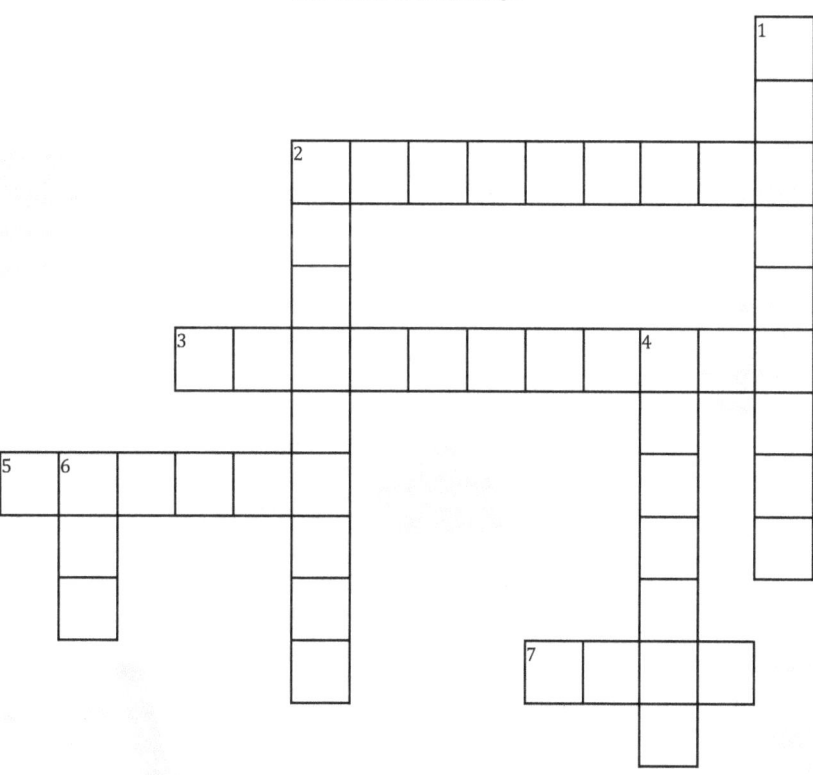

Across

2. A large reptile with short legs, a long body and tail, and a long, wide snout. _____s are protected by thick skin with many hard bumps. They live in rivers, lakes, swamps, and other bodies of water in the southeast united states and in china.

3. An insect with long, powerful hind legs for jumping and two pairs of wings. _____s eat plants.

5. _____s are mammals known for their powerful digging. They are related to weasels, skunks, otters, and mink. _____s live in many habitats, including grasslands.

7. A tiny insect that does not have wings but can jump far. _____s feed on the blood of the animals they bite.

Down

1. Any of several dark-colored, long-necked seabirds having a hooked bill and an expandable food pouch, often brightly colored, under the bill.

2. A very large sea bird found mostly in the southern hemisphere. _____es have webbed feet, long narrow wings, and hooked beaks.

4. A leopard, especially a black one with no spots that show. Leopards live in Africa and Asia. They are carnivorous mammals and are closely related to lions, tigers, and other large cats that roar.

6. A small insect, often red or black. _____s live in large groups in the ground.

Kitchen

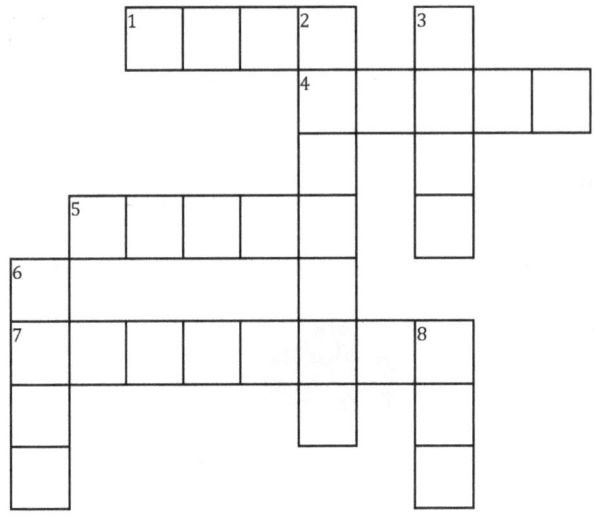

Across

1. _____s get very hot. You can bake food in an _____.

4. _____s are sharp tasting vegetables.

5. A _____ is a type of food that is usually made with lettuce and other vegetables.

7. _____ is cold, creamy, and sweet treat.

Down

2. _____ a flat, narrow strip of dough that has been dried. _____ are boiled in water to make them soft for eating.

3. A _____ is a sour, green citrus fruit.

6. _____ comes from cows and other mammals.

8. A _____ is a large cup.

Conclusion

Thank you again for buying this book!   I hope you enjoyed with my book. Finally, if you like this book, please take the time to share your thoughts and post a review on Amazon. It'd be greatly appreciated! Thank you!

Next Steps
– Write me an honest review about the book –
I truly value your opinion and thoughts and I will incorporate them into my next book, which is already underway.

Get more free bonus here

www.funspace.club

Follow us : facebook.com/funspaceclub

Send email to get answer & solution here : funspaceclub18@gmail.com

Find us on Amazon

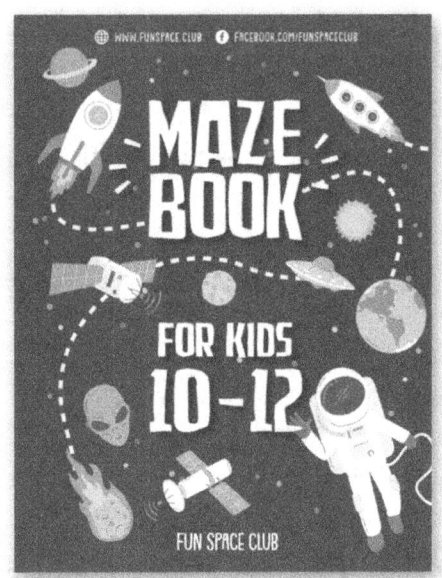
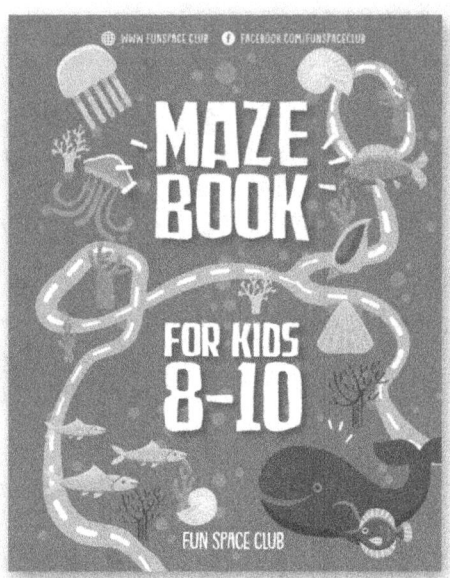

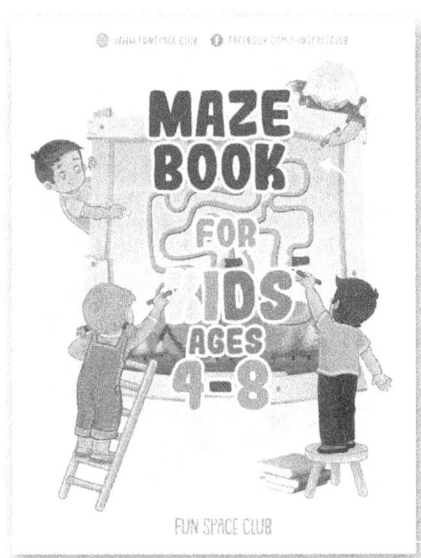
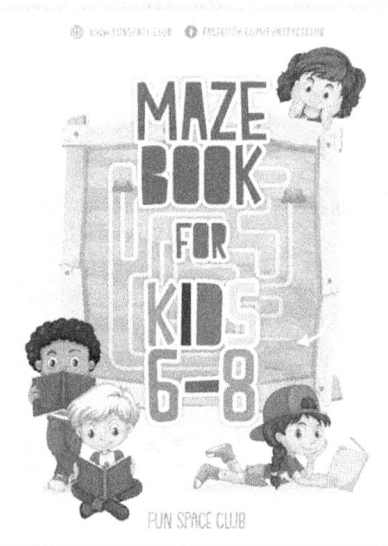
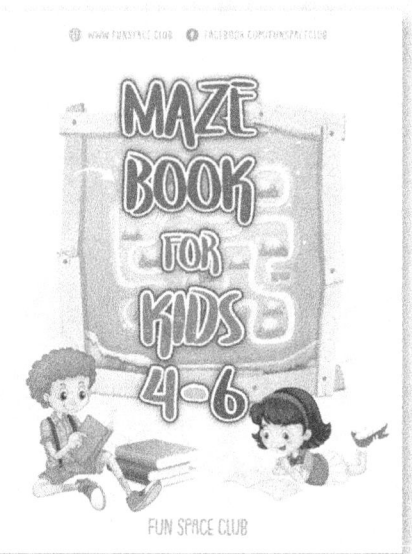

Find us on Amazon

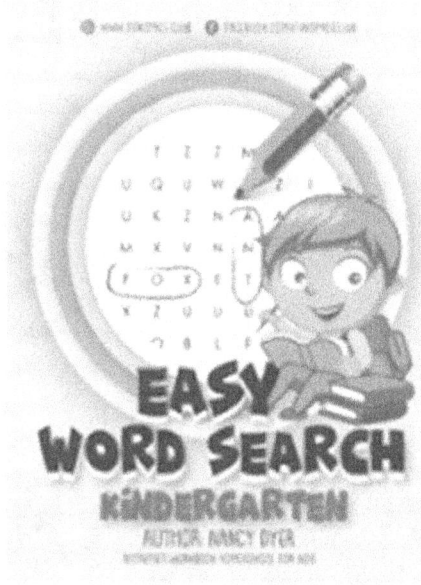

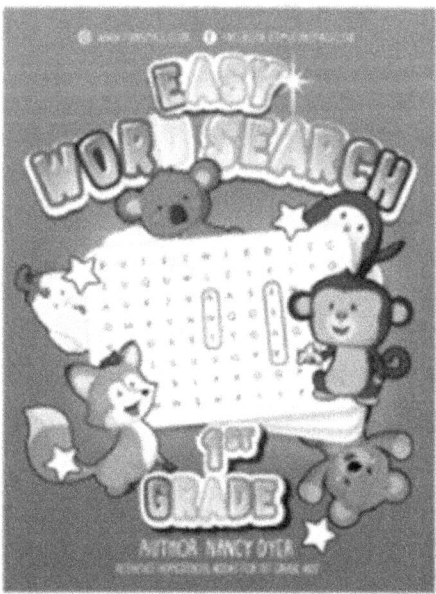

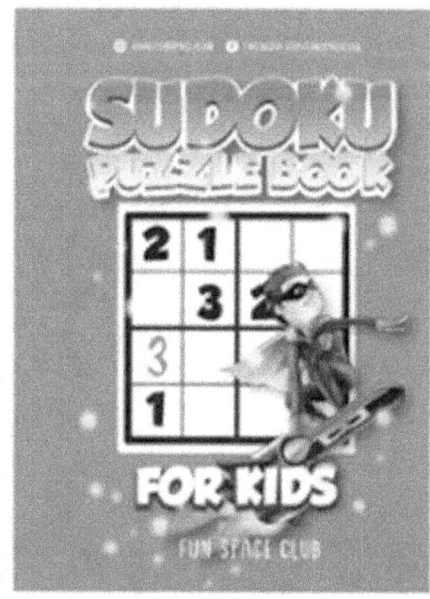

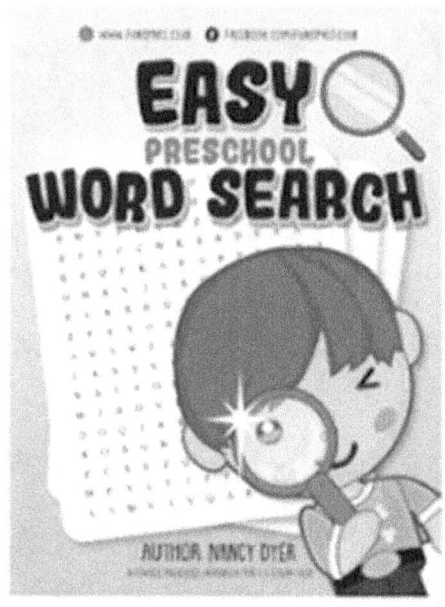

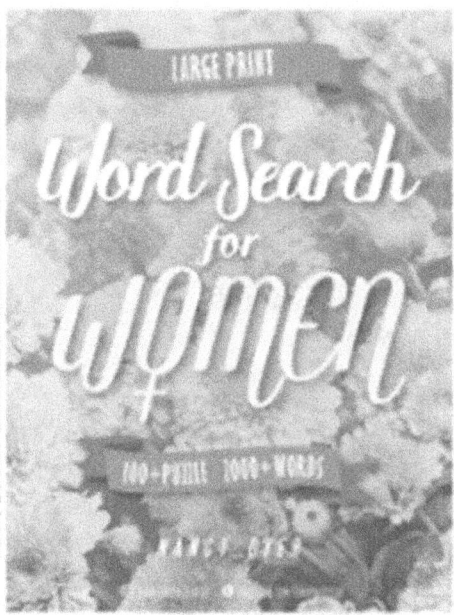

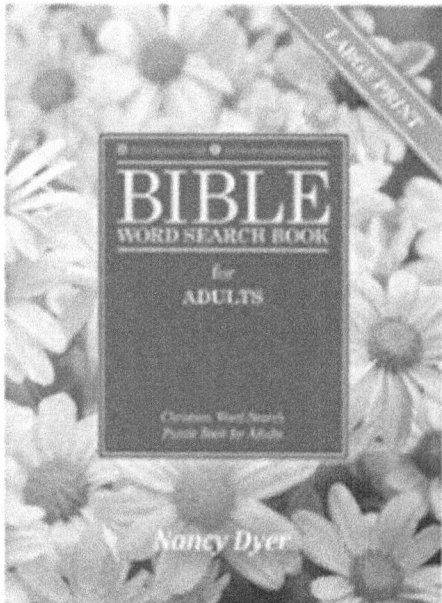